PEARSON

COMMON CORE

Literature

Close Reading Notebook

GRADE 6

PEARSON

UPPER SADDLE RIVER, NEW JERSEY • BOSTON, MASSACHUSETTS
CHANDLER, ARIZONA • GLENVIEW, ILLINOIS

Acknowledgments appear on page 155, which constitutes an extension of this copyright page.

PEARSON

ISBN-13: 978-0-13-327565-0
ISBN-10: 0-13-327565-5
2 3 4 5 6 7 8 9 10 V039 17 16 15 14 13

CONTENTS

UNIT 1

UNIT 2

UNIT 3

UNIT 4

UNIT 5

The Wounded Wolf

by Jean Craighead George

TAKE NOTES

A wounded wolf climbs Toklat Ridge,[1] a massive spine of rock and ice. As he limps, dawn strikes the ridge and lights it up with sparks and stars. Roko, the wounded wolf, blinks in the ice fire, then stops to rest and watch his pack run the thawing Arctic valley.

They plunge and turn. They fight the mighty caribou that struck young Roko with his hoof and wounded him. He jumped between the beast and Kiglo, leader of the Toklat pack. Young Roko spun and fell. Hooves, paws, and teeth roared over him. And then his pack and the beast were gone.

Gravely injured, Roko pulls himself toward the shelter rock. Weakness overcomes him. He stops. He and his pack are thin and hungry. This is the season of starvation. The winter's harvest has been taken. The produce of spring has not begun.

Young Roko glances down the valley. He droops his head and stiffens his tail to signal to his pack that he is badly hurt. Winds wail. A frigid blast picks up long shawls of snow and drapes them between young Roko and his pack. And so his message is not read.

A raven scouting Toklat Ridge sees Roko's signal. "Kong, kong, kong," he bells—death is coming to the ridge; there will be flesh and bone for all. His voice rolls out across the valley. It penetrates the rocky cracks where the Toklat ravens rest. One by one they hear and spread their wings. They beat their way to Toklat Ridge. They alight upon the snow and walk behind the wounded wolf.

"Kong," they toll[2] with keen excitement, for the raven clan is hungry, too. "Kong, kong"—there will be flesh and bone for all. Roko snarls and hurries toward the shelter rock. A cloud of snow envelops him. He limps in blinding whiteness now. A ghostly presence flits

1. **Toklat Ridge** the top of a mountain located in Alaska's Denali National Park and Preserve.
2. **toll** (tōl) *v.* announce.

TAKE NOTES

around. "Hahahahahahaha," the white fox states—death is coming to the Ridge. Roko smells the fox tagging at his heels.

The cloud whirls off. Two golden eyes look up at Roko. The snowy owl has heard the ravens and joined the deathwatch.

Roko limps along. The ravens walk. The white fox leaps. The snowy owl flies and hops along the rim of Toklat Ridge. Roko stops. Below the ledge out on the flats the musk-ox herd is circling. They form a ring and all face out, a fort of heads and horns and fur that sweeps down to their hooves. Their circle means to Roko that an enemy is present. He squints and smells the wind. It carries scents of thawing ice, broken grass—and earth. The grizzly bear is up! He has awakened from his winter's sleep. A craving need for flesh will drive him.

Roko sees the shelter rock. He strains to reach it. He stumbles. The ravens move in closer. The white fox boldly walks beside him. "Hahaha," he yaps. The snowy owl flies ahead, alights, and waits.

The grizzly hears the eager fox and rises on his flat hind feet. He twists his powerful neck and head. His great paws dangle at his chest. He sees the animal procession and hears the ravens' knell[3] of death. Dropping to all fours, he joins the march up Toklat Ridge.

Roko stops; his breath comes hard. A raven alights upon his back and picks the open wound. Roko snaps. The raven flies and circles back. The white fox nips at Roko's toes. The snowy owl inches closer. The grizzly bear, still dulled by sleep, stumbles onto Toklat Ridge.

Only yards from the shelter rock, Roko falls.

Instantly the ravens mob him. They scream and peck and stab at his eyes. The white fox leaps upon his wound. The snowy owl sits and waits.

Young Roko struggles to his feet. He bites the ravens. Snaps the fox. And lunges at the stoic[4] owl. He turns and warns the grizzly bear. Then he bursts into a run and falls against the shelter rock. The wounded wolf

---

3. **knell** (nel) *n.* mournful sound, like a slowly ringing bell—usually indicating a death.
4. **stoic** (stō´ ik) *adj.* calm and unaffected by hardship.

wedges down between the rock and barren ground. Now protected on three sides, he turns and faces all his foes.

The ravens step a few feet closer. The fox slides toward him on his belly. The snowy owl blinks and waits, and on the ridge rim roars the hungry grizzly bear.

Roko growls.

The sun comes up. Far across the Toklat Valley, Roko hears his pack's "hunt's end" song. The music wails and sobs, wilder than the bleating wind. The hunt song ends. Next comes the roll call. Each member of the Toklat pack barks to say that he is home and well.

"Kiglo here," Roko hears his leader bark. There is a pause. It is young Roko's turn. He cannot lift his head to answer: the pack is silent. The leader starts the count once more. "Kiglo here."—a pause. Roko cannot answer.

The wounded wolf whimpers softly. A mindful raven hears. "Kong, kong, kong," he tolls—this is the end. His booming sounds across the valley. The wolf pack hears the raven's message that something is dying. They know it is Roko, who has not answered roll call.

The hours pass. The wind slams snow on Toklat Ridge. Massive clouds blot out the sun. In their gloom Roko sees the deathwatch move in closer. Suddenly he hears the musk-oxen thundering into their circle. The ice cracks as the grizzly leaves. The ravens burst into the air. The white fox runs. The snowy owl flaps to the top of the shelter rock. And Kiglo rounds the knoll.

In his mouth he carries meat. He drops it close to Roko's head and wags his tail excitedly. Roko licks Kiglo's chin to honor him. Then Kiglo puts his mouth around Roko's nose. This gesture says "I am your leader." And by mouthing Roko, he binds him and all the wolves together.

The wounded wolf wags his tail. Kiglo trots away.

Already Roko's wound feels better. He gulps the food and feels his strength return. He shatters bone, flesh, and gristle and shakes the scraps out on the snow. The hungry ravens swoop upon them. The white fox snatches up a bone. The snowy owl gulps down flesh and fur. And Roko wags his tail and watches.

TAKE NOTES

TAKE NOTES

For days Kiglo brings young Roko food. He gnashes, gorges, and shatters bits upon the snow.

A purple sandpiper winging north sees ravens, owl, and fox. And he drops in upon the feast. The long-tailed jaeger gull flies down and joins the crowd on Toklat Ridge. Roko wags his tail.

One dawn he moves his wounded leg. He stretches it and pulls himself into the sunlight. He walks—he romps. He runs in circles. He leaps and plays with chunks of ice. Suddenly he stops. The "hunt's end" song rings out. Next comes the roll call.

"Kiglo here."

"Roko here," he barks out strongly.

The pack is silent.

"Kiglo here," the leader repeats.

"Roko here."

Across the distance comes the sound of whoops and yips and barks and howls. They fill the dawn with celebration. And Roko prances down the Ridge.

Stray

by Cynthia Rylant

TAKE NOTES

In January, a puppy wandered onto the property of Mr. Amos Lacey and his wife, Mamie, and their daughter, Doris. Icicles hung three feet or more from the eaves of houses, snowdrifts swallowed up automobiles and the birds were so fluffed up they looked comic.

The puppy had been abandoned, and it made its way down the road toward the Laceys' small house, its ears tucked, its tail between its legs, shivering.

Doris, whose school had been called off because of the snow, was out shoveling the cinderblock front steps when she spotted the pup on the road. She set down the shovel.

"Hey! Come on!" she called.

The puppy stopped in the road, wagging its tail timidly, trembling with shyness and cold.

Doris trudged through the yard, went up the shoveled drive and met the dog.

"Come on, Pooch."

"Where did *that* come from?" Mrs. Lacey asked as soon as Doris put the dog down in the kitchen.

Mr. Lacey was at the table, cleaning his fingernails with his pocketknife. The snow was keeping him home from his job at the warehouse.

"I don't know where it came from," he said mildly, "but I know for sure where it's going."

Doris hugged the puppy hard against her. She said nothing.

Because the roads would be too bad for travel for many days, Mr. Lacey couldn't get out to take the puppy to the pound[1] in the city right away. He agreed to let it sleep in the basement while Mrs. Lacey grudgingly let Doris feed it table scraps. The woman was sensitive about throwing out food.

1. **pound** (pound) *n.* animal shelter.

TAKE NOTES

By the looks of it, Doris figured the puppy was about six months old, and on its way to being a big dog. She thought it might have some shepherd in it. •

Four days passed and the puppy did not complain. It never cried in the night or howled at the wind. It didn't tear up everything in the basement. It wouldn't even follow Doris up the basement steps unless it was invited.

It was a good dog.

Several times Doris had opened the door in the kitchen that led to the basement and the puppy had been there, all stretched out, on the top step. Doris knew it had wanted some company and that it had lain against the door, listening to the talk in the kitchen, smelling the food, being a part of things. It always wagged its tail, eyes all sleepy, when she found it there.

Even after a week had gone by, Doris didn't name the dog. She knew her parents wouldn't let her keep it, that her father made so little money any pets were out of the question, and that the pup would definitely go to the pound when the weather cleared.

Still, she tried talking to them about the dog at dinner one night.

"She's a good dog, isn't she?" Doris said, hoping one of them would agree with her.

Her parents glanced at each other and went on eating.

"She's not much trouble," Doris added. "I like her." She smiled at them, but they continued to ignore her.

"I figure she's real smart," Doris said to her mother. "I could teach her things."

Mrs. Lacey just shook her head and stuffed a forkful of sweet potato in her mouth. Doris fell silent, praying the weather would never clear.

But on Saturday, nine days after the dog had arrived, the sun was shining and the roads were plowed. Mr. Lacey opened up the trunk of his car and came into the house.

Doris was sitting alone in the living room, hugging a pillow and rocking back and forth on the edge of a chair. She was trying not to cry but she was not strong enough. Her face was wet and red, her eyes full of distress.

Mrs. Lacey looked into the room from the doorway.

"Mama," Doris said in a small voice. "Please."

Mrs. Lacey shook her head.

"You know we can't afford a dog, Doris. You try to act more grown-up about this."

Doris pressed her face into the pillow.

Outside, she heard the trunk of the car slam shut, one of the doors open and close, the old engine cough and choke and finally start up.

"Daddy," she whispered. "Please."

She heard the car travel down the road, and, though it was early afternoon, she could do nothing but go to her bed. She cried herself to sleep, and her dreams were full of searching and searching for things lost. ●

It was nearly night when she finally woke up. Lying there, like stone, still exhausted, she wondered if she would ever in her life have anything. She stared at the wall for a while.

But she started feeling hungry, and she knew she'd have to make herself get out of bed and eat some dinner. She wanted not to go into the kitchen, past the basement door. She wanted not to face her parents.

But she rose up heavily.

Her parents were sitting at the table, dinner over, drinking coffee. They looked at her when she came in, but she kept her head down. No one spoke.

Doris made herself a glass of powdered milk and drank it all down. Then she picked up a cold biscuit and started out of the room.

"You'd better feed that mutt before it dies of starvation," Mr. Lacey said.

Doris turned around.

"What?"

"I said, you'd better feed your dog. I figure it's looking for you."

Doris put her hand to her mouth.

"You didn't take her?" she asked.

"Oh, I took her all right," her father answered. "Worst looking place I've ever seen. Ten dogs to a cage. Smell was enough to knock you down. And they give an animal six days to live. Then they kill it with some kind of a shot."

Doris stared at her father.

TAKE NOTES

TAKE NOTES

"I wouldn't leave an ant in that place," he said. "So I brought the dog back."

Mrs. Lacey was smiling at him and shaking her head as if she would never, ever, understand him.

Mr. Lacey sipped his coffee.

"Well," he said, "are you going to feed it or not?"

The Tail

by Joyce Hansen

TAKE NOTES

It began as the worst summer of my life. The evening before the first day of summer vacation, my mother broke the bad news to me. I was in the kitchen washing dishes and dreaming about the wonderful things my friends and I would be doing for two whole months—practicing for the annual double-dutch[1] contest, which we would definitely win; going to the roller skating rink, the swimming pool, the beach; and sleeping as late in the morning as I wanted to.

"Tasha," my ma broke into my happy thoughts, "your father and I decided that you're old enough now to take on certain responsibilities."

My heart came to a sudden halt. "Responsibilities?"

"Yes. You do know what that word means, don't you?"

I nodded, watching her dice an onion into small, perfect pieces.

"You're thirteen going on fourteen and your father and I decided that you're old enough to watch Junior this summer, because I'm going to start working again."

"Oh, no!" I broke the dish with a crash. "Not that, Mama." Junior is my seven-year-old brother and has been following me like a tail ever since he learned how to walk. And to make matters worse, there are no kids Junior's age on our block. Everyone is either older or younger than he is.

I'd rather be in school than minding Junior all day. I could've cried.

"Natasha! There won't be a dish left in this house. You're not going to spend all summer ripping and roaring. You'll baby-sit Junior."

"But, Ma," I said, "it'll be miserable. That's not fair. All summer with Junior. I won't be able to play with my friends."

1. **double-dutch** a jump-rope game in which two ropes are used at the same time.

TAKE NOTES

She wiped her hands on her apron. “Life ain’t always fair.”

I knew she’d say that.

“You’ll still be able to play with your friends,” she continued, “but Junior comes first. He is your responsibility. We’re a family and we all have to help out.” •

Mama went to work that next morning. Junior and I both stood by the door as she gave her last-minute instructions. Junior held her hand and stared up at her with an innocent look in his bright brown eyes, which everyone thought were so cute. Dimples decorated his round cheeks as he smiled and nodded at me every time Ma gave me an order. I knew he was just waiting for her to leave so he could torment me.

“Tasha, I’m depending on you. Don’t leave the block.”

“Yes, Ma.”

“No company.”

“Not even Naomi? She’s my best friend.”

“No company when your father and I are not home.”

“Yes, Ma.”

“Don’t let Junior hike in the park.”

“Yes, Ma.”

“Make yourself and Junior a sandwich for lunch.”

“Yes, Ma.”

“I’ll be calling you at twelve, so you’d better be in here fixing lunch. I don’t want you all eating junk food all day long.”

“Yes, Ma.”

“Don’t ignore Junior.”

“Yes, Ma.”

“Clean the breakfast dishes.”

“Yes, Ma.”

“Don’t open the door to strangers.”

“Yes, Ma.”

Then she turned to Junior. “Now you, young man. You are to listen to your sister.”

“Yes, Mommy,” he sang out.

“Don’t give her a hard time. Show me what a big boy you can be.”

“Mommy, I’ll do whatever Tasha say.”

She kissed us both good-bye and left. I wanted to cry. A whole summer with Junior.

Junior turned to me and raised his right hand. "This is a vow of obedience." He looked up at the ceiling. "I promise to do whatever Tasha says."

"What do you know about vows?" I asked.

"I saw it on television. A man—"

"Shut up, Junior. I don't feel like hearing about some television show. It's too early in the morning."

I went into the kitchen to start cleaning, when the downstairs bell rang. "Answer the intercom,[2] Junior. If it's Naomi, tell her to wait for me on the stoop," I called out. I knew that it was Naomi, ready to start our big, fun summer. After a few minutes the bell rang again.

"Junior!" I yelled. "Answer the intercom."

The bell rang again and I ran into the living room. Junior was sitting on the couch, looking at cartoons. "What's wrong with you? Why won't you answer the bell?"

He looked at me as if I were crazy. "You told me to shut up. I told you I'd do everything you say."

I pulled my hair. "See, you're bugging me already. Do something to help around here."

I pressed the intercom on the wall. "That you, Naomi?"

"Yeah."

"I'll be down in a minute. Wait for me out front."

"Okay."

I quickly washed the dishes. I couldn't believe how messed up my plans were. Suddenly there was a loud blast from the living room. I was so startled that I dropped a plate and it smashed to smithereens. Ma will kill me, I thought as I ran to the living room. It sounded like whole pieces of furniture were being sucked into the vacuum cleaner.

"Junior," I screamed over the racket, "you have it on too high."

He couldn't even hear me. I turned it off myself.

"What's wrong?"

"Ma vacuumed the living room last night. It doesn't need cleaning."

"You told me to do something to help," he whined.

TAKE NOTES

2. **intercom** *n.* a communication system used in apartment buildings.

TAKE NOTES

I finished the dishes in a hurry so that I could leave the apartment before Junior bugged out again. •

I was so anxious to get outside that we ran down the four flights of stairs instead of waiting for the elevator. Junior clutched some comic books and his checkers game. He put his Mets baseball cap on backward as usual. Naomi sat on the stoop and Junior plopped right next to her like they were the best of friends.

"Hi, cutey." She smiled at him, turning his cap to the front of his head the way it was supposed to be.

"What are we going to do today, Naomi?" he asked.

"Junior, you're not going to be in our faces all day," I snapped at him.

"Mama said you have to watch me. So I have to be in your face."

"You're baby-sitting, Tasha?" Naomi asked.

"Yeah." I told her the whole story.

"Aw, that's not so bad. At least you don't have to stay in the house. Junior will be good. Right, cutey?"

He grinned as she pinched his cheeks.

"See, you think he's cute because you don't have no pesty little brother or sister to watch," I grumbled.

"You ready for double-dutch practice?" she asked. "Yvonne and Keisha are going to meet us in the playground."

"Mama said we have to stay on the block," Junior answered before I could even open my mouth.

"No one's talking to you, Junior." I pulled Naomi up off the stoop. "I promised my mother we'd stay on the block, but the playground is just across the street. I can see the block from there."

"It's still not the block," Junior mumbled as we raced across the street.

We always went over to the playground to jump rope. The playground was just by the entrance to the park. There was a lot of space for us to do our fancy steps. The park was like a big green mountain in the middle of Broadway.

I'd figure out a way to keep Junior from telling that we really didn't stay on the block. "Hey, Tasha, can I go inside the park and look for caves?" People said that if you went deep inside the park, there were caves that had been used centuries ago when Native Americans still lived in northern Manhattan.

"No, Ma said no hiking in the park."

"She said no leaving the block, too, and you left the block."

"Look how close we are to the block. I mean, we can even see it. You could get lost inside the park."

"I'm going to tell Ma you didn't stay on the block."

"Okay, me and Naomi will hike with you up to the Cloisters later." That's a museum that sits at the top of the park, overlooking the Hudson River. "Now read your comic books."

"Will you play checkers with me too?"

"You know I hate checkers. Leave me alone."

I spotted Keisha and Yvonne walking into the playground. All of us wore shorts and sneakers.

Junior tagged behind me and Naomi as we went to meet them. "Remember you're supposed to be watching me," he said.

"How could I forget."

The playground was crowded. Swings were all taken and the older boys played stickball. Some little kids played in the sandboxes.

Keisha and Yvonne turned and Naomi and I jumped together, practicing a new routine. We were so good that some of the boys in the stickball game watched us. A few elderly people stopped to look at us too. We had an audience, so I really showed off—spinning and doing a lot of fancy footwork.

Suddenly Junior jumped in the ropes with us and people laughed and clapped.

"Junior!" I screamed. "Get out of here!"

"Remember, your job is to watch me." He grinned. My foot slipped and all three of us got tangled in the ropes and fell.

"Your feet are too big!" Junior yelled.

Everybody roared. I was too embarrassed. I tried to grab him, but he got away from me. "Get lost," I hollered after him as he ran toward the swings.

I tried to forget how stupid I must've looked and went back to the ropes. I don't know how long we'd been jumping when suddenly a little kid ran by us yelling,

TAKE NOTES

TAKE NOTES

"There's a wild dog loose up there!" He pointed to the steps that led deep inside the park.

People had been saying for years that a pack of abandoned dogs who'd turned wild lived in the park, but no one ever really saw them.

We forgot about the kid and kept jumping. Then one of the boys our age who'd been playing stickball came over to us. "We're getting out of here," he said. "A big yellow dog with red eyes just bit a kid."

I took the rope from Yvonne. It was time for me and Naomi to turn. "That's ridiculous. Who ever heard of a yellow dog with red eyes?"

Naomi stopped turning. "Dogs look all kind of ways. Especially wild dogs. I'm leaving."

"Me too," Yvonne said.

Keisha was already gone. No one was in the swings or the sandboxes. I didn't even see the old men who usually sat on the benches. "Guess we'd better get out of here too," I said. Then I realized that I didn't see Junior anywhere.

"Junior!" I shouted.

"Maybe he went home," Naomi said.

We dashed across the street. Our block was empty. Yvonne ran ahead of us and didn't stop until she reached her stoop. When I got to my stoop I expected to see Junior there, but no Junior.

"Maybe he went upstairs," Naomi said.

"I have the key. He can't get in the house."

"Maybe he went to the candy store?"

"He doesn't have any money, I don't think. But let's look."

We ran around the corner to the candy store, but no Junior.

As we walked back to the block, I remembered something.

"Oh, no, Naomi, I told him to get lost. And that's just what he did."

"He's probably hiding from us somewhere. You know how he likes to tease." She looked around as we walked up our block. "He might be hiding and watching us right now looking for him." She peeped behind parked cars, in doorways, and even opened the lid of a trash can.

"Junior," I called. "Junior!"

No answer. Only the sounds of birds and cars, sirens and a distant radio. I looked at the empty stoop where Junior should have been sitting. A part of me was gone and I had to find it. And another part of me would be gone if my mother found out I'd lost Junior.

I ran back toward the playground and Naomi followed me. "He's got to be somewhere right around here," she panted.

I ran past the playground and into the park. "Tasha, you're not going in there, are you? The dog."

I didn't answer her and began climbing the stone steps that wound around and through the park. Naomi's eyes stretched all over her face and she grabbed my arm. "It's dangerous up here!"

I turned around. "If you're scared, don't come. Junior's my only baby brother. Dear God," I said out loud, "please let me find him. I will play any kind of game he wants. I'll never yell at him again. I promise never to be mean to him again in my life!"

Naomi breathed heavily behind me. "I don't think Junior would go this far by himself."

I stopped and caught my breath. The trees were thick and the city street sounds were far away now.

"I know Junior. He's somewhere up here making believe he's the king of this mountain. Hey, Junior," I called, "I was just kidding. Don't get lost." We heard a rustling in the bushes and grabbed each other. "Probably just a bird," I said, trying to sound brave.

As we climbed some more, I tried not to imagine a huge yellow dog with red eyes gnawing at my heels.

The steps turned a corner and ended. Naomi screamed and pointed up ahead. "What's that?"

I saw a big brown and gray monstrous thing with tentacles reaching toward the sky, jutting out of the curve in the path. I screamed and almost ran.

"What is that, Naomi?"

"I don't know."

"This is a park in the middle of Manhattan. It can't be a bear or anything." I screamed to the top of my lungs, "Junior!" Some birds flew out of a tree, but the thing never moved.

All Naomi could say was, "Dogs, Tasha."

I found a stick. "I'm going up. You wait here. If you hear growling and screaming, run and get some help."

TAKE NOTES

TAKE NOTES

I couldn't believe how brave I was. Anyway, that thing, whatever it was, couldn't hurt me any more than my mother would if I didn't find Junior.

"You sure, Tasha?"

"No sense in both of us being mauled," I said.

I tipped lightly up the steps, holding the stick like a club. When I was a few feet away from the thing, I crumpled to the ground and laughed so hard that Naomi ran to me. "Naomi, look at what scared us."

She laughed too. "A dead tree trunk."

We both laughed until we cried. Then I saw one of Junior's comic books near a bush. I picked it up and started to cry. "See, he was here. And that animal probably tore him to pieces." Naomi patted my shaking shoulders.

Suddenly, there was an unbelievable growl. My legs turned to air as I flew down the steps. Naomi was ahead of me. Her two braids stuck out like propellers. My feet didn't even touch the ground. We screamed all the way down the steps. I tripped on the last step and was sprawled out on the ground. Two women passing by bent over me. "Child, are you hurt?" one of them asked.

Then I heard a familiar laugh above me and looked up into Junior's dimpled face. He laughed so hard, he held his stomach with one hand. His checkers game was in the other. A little tan, mangy[3] dog stood next to him, wagging its tail.

I got up slowly. "Junior, I'm going to choke you."

He doubled over with squeals and chuckles. I wiped my filthy shorts with one hand and stretched out the other to snatch Junior's neck. The stupid little dog had the nerve to growl.

"Me and Thunder hid in the bushes. We followed you." He continued laughing. Then he turned to the dog. "Thunder, didn't Tasha look funny holding that stick like she was going to beat up the tree trunk?"

I put my hands around Junior's neck. "This is the end of the tail," I said.

Junior grinned. "You promised. 'I'll play any game he wants. I'll never yell at him again. I promise never to be mean to him again in my life.' "

---

3. mangy (mān´ jē) *adj.* shabby and dirty.

Naomi giggled. "That's what you said, Tasha." The mutt barked at me. Guess he called himself Junior's protector. I took my hands off Junior's neck.

Then Naomi had a laughing spasm. She pointed at the dog. "Is that what everyone was running from?"

"This is my trusted guard. People say he's wild. He just wants a friend."

"Thunder looks like he's already got a lot of friends living inside his fur," I said. We walked back to the block with the dog trotting right by Junior's side.

I checked my watch when we got to my building. "It's ten to twelve. I have to make lunch for Junior," I told Naomi. "But I'll be back out later."

The dog whined after Junior as we entered the building. "I'll be back soon, Thunder," he said, "after I beat my sister in five games of checkers."

Now he was going to blackmail me.

I heard Naomi giggling as Junior and I walked into the building. The phone rang just as we entered the apartment. I knew it was Ma.

"Everything okay, Tasha? Nothing happened?"

"No, Ma, everything is fine. Nothing happened at all." •

Well, the summer didn't turn out to be so terrible after all. My parents got Thunder cleaned up and let Junior keep him for a pet. Me and my friends practiced for the double-dutch contest right in front of my building, so I didn't have to leave the block. After lunch when it was too hot to jump rope, I'd play a game of checkers with Junior or read him a story. He wasn't as pesty as he used to be, because now he had Thunder. We won the double-dutch contest. And Junior never told my parents that I'd lost him. I found out that you never miss a tail until you almost lose it.

TAKE NOTES

TAKE NOTES

The King of Mazy May

by Jack London

Walt Masters is not a very large boy, but there is manliness in his make-up, and he himself, although he does not know a great deal that most boys know, knows much that other boys do not know. He has never seen a train of cars nor an elevator in his life, and for that matter he has never once looked upon a cornfield, a plow, a cow, or even a chicken. He has never had a pair of shoes on his feet, nor gone to a picnic or a party, nor talked to a girl. But he has seen the sun at midnight, watched the ice jams on one of the mightiest of rivers, and played beneath the northern lights,[1] the one white child in thousands of square miles of frozen wilderness.

Walt has walked all the fourteen years of his life in suntanned, moose-hide moccasins, and he can go to the Indian camps and "talk big" with the men, and trade calico and beads with them for their precious furs. He can make bread without baking powder, yeast, or hops, shoot a moose at three hundred yards, and drive the wild wolf dogs fifty miles a day on the packed trail.

Last of all, he has a good heart, and is not afraid of the darkness and loneliness, of man or beast or thing. His father is a good man, strong and brave, and Walt is growing up like him.

Walt was born a thousand miles or so down the Yukon,[2] in a trading post below the Ramparts. After his mother died, his father and he came up on the river, step by step, from camp to camp, till now they are settled down on the Mazy May Creek in the Klondike country. Last year they and several others had spent much toil and time on the Mazy May, and endured great hardships; the creek, in turn, was just beginning to show up its richness and to reward them for their

1. **northern lights** glowing bands or streamers of light, sometimes appearing in the night sky of the Northern Hemisphere.
2. **Yukon** (yo͞o´ kän´) river flowing through the Yukon Territory of northwest Canada.

heavy labor. But with the news of their discoveries, strange men began to come and go through the short days and long nights, and many unjust things they did to the men who had worked so long upon the creek.

Si Hartman had gone away on a moose hunt, to return and find new stakes driven and his claim jumped.[3] George Lukens and his brother had lost their claims in a like manner, having delayed too long on the way to Dawson to record them. In short, it was the old story, and quite a number of the earnest, industrious prospectors had suffered similar losses.

But Walt Masters's father had recorded his claim at the start, so Walt had nothing to fear now that his father had gone on a short trip up the White River prospecting for quartz. Walt was well able to stay by himself in the cabin, cook his three meals a day, and look after things. Not only did he look after his father's claim, but he had agreed to keep an eye on the adjoining one of Loren Hall, who had started for Dawson to record it.

Loren Hall was an old man, and he had no dogs, so he had to travel very slowly. After he had been gone some time, word came up the river that he had broken through the ice at Rosebud Creek and frozen his feet so badly that he would not be able to travel for a couple of weeks. Then Walt Masters received the news that old Loren was nearly all right again, and about to move on afoot for Dawson as fast as a weakened man could.

Walt was worried, however; the claim was liable to be jumped at any moment because of this delay, and a fresh stampede had started in on the Mazy May. He did not like the looks of the newcomers, and one day, when five of them came by with crack dog teams and the lightest of camping outfits, he could see that they were prepared to make speed, and resolved to keep an eye on them. So he locked up the cabin and followed them, being at the same time careful to remain hidden.

He had not watched them long before he was sure that they were professional stampeders, bent on jumping all the claims in sight. Walt crept along the snow at the rim of the creek and saw them change many stakes, destroy old ones, and set up new ones.

TAKE NOTES

3. **claim jumped** A claim is a piece of land marked by a miner with stakes to show where the borders are. A claim that is jumped is stolen by someone else.

TAKE NOTES

In the afternoon, with Walt always trailing on their heels, they came back down the creek, unharnessed their dogs, and went into camp within two claims of his cabin. When he saw them make preparations to cook, he hurried home to get something to eat himself, and then hurried back. He crept so close that he could hear them talking quite plainly, and by pushing the underbrush aside he could catch occasional glimpses of them. They had finished eating and were smoking around the fire.

"The creek is all right, boys," a large, black-bearded man, evidently the leader, said, "and I think the best thing we can do is to pull out tonight. The dogs can follow the trail; besides, it's going to be moonlight. What say you?"

"But it's going to be beastly cold," objected one of the party. "It's forty below zero now."

"An' sure, can't ye keep warm by jumpin' off the sleds an' runnin' after the dogs?" cried an Irishman. "An' who wouldn't? The creek's as rich as a United States mint! Faith, it's an ilegant chanst to be gettin' a run fer yer money! An' if ye don't run, it's mebbe you'll not get the money at all, at all."

"That's it," said the leader. "If we can get to Dawson and record, we're rich men; and there's no telling who's been sneaking along in our tracks, watching us, and perhaps now off to give the alarm. The thing for us to do is to rest the dogs a bit, and then hit the trail as hard as we can. What do you say?"

Evidently the men had agreed with their leader, for Walt Masters could hear nothing but the rattle of the tin dishes which were being washed. Peering out cautiously, he could see the leader studying a piece of paper. Walt knew what it was at a glance—a list of all the unrecorded claims on Mazy May. Any man could get these lists by applying to the gold commissioner at Dawson.

"Thirty-two," the leader said, lifting his face to the men. "Thirty-two isn't recorded, and this is thirty-three. Come on; let's take a look at it. I saw somebody had been working on it when we came up this morning."

Three of the men went with him, leaving one to remain in camp. Walt crept carefully after them till they came to Loren Hall's shaft. One of the men went down and built a fire on the bottom to thaw out the frozen gravel, while the others built another fire on the dump and melted water in a couple of gold pans. This they poured into a piece of canvas stretched between two logs, used by Loren Hall in which to wash his gold.

In a short time a couple of buckets of dirt were sent up by the man in the shaft, and Walt could see the others grouped anxiously about their leader as he proceeded to wash it. When this was finished, they stared at the broad streak of black sand and yellow gold grains on the bottom of the pan, and one of them called excitedly for the man who had remained in camp to come. Loren Hall had struck it rich and his claim was not yet recorded. It was plain that they were going to jump it.

Walt lay in the snow, thinking rapidly. He was only a boy, but in the face of the threatened injustice to old lame Loren Hall he felt that he must do something. He waited and watched, with his mind made up, till he saw the men begin to square up new stakes. Then he crawled away till out of hearing, and broke into a run for the camp of the stampeders. Walt's father had taken their own dogs with him prospecting, and the boy knew how impossible it was for him to undertake the seventy miles to Dawson without the aid of dogs.

Gaining the camp, he picked out, with an experienced eye, the easiest running sled and started to harness up the stampeders' dogs. There were three teams of six each, and from these he chose ten of the best. Realizing how necessary it was to have a good head dog, he strove to discover a leader amongst them; but he had little time in which to do it, for he could hear the voices of the returning men. By the time the team was in shape and everything ready, the claim-jumpers came into sight in an open place not more than a hundred yards from the trail, which ran down the bed of the creek. They cried out to Walt, but instead of giving heed to them he grabbed up one of their fur sleeping robes, which lay loosely in the snow, and leaped upon the sled.

"Mush! Hi! Mush on!" he cried to the animals, snapping the keen-lashed whip among them.

The dogs sprang against the yoke straps, and the sled jerked under way so suddenly as to almost

TAKE NOTES

TAKE NOTES

throw him off. Then it curved into the creek, poising perilously on the runner. He was almost breathless with suspense, when it finally righted with a bound and sprang ahead again. The creek bank was high and he could not see the men, although he could hear their cries and knew they were running to cut him off. He did not dare to think what would happen if they caught him; he just clung to the sled, his heart beating wildly, and watched the snow rim of the bank above him.

Suddenly, over this snow rim came the flying body of the Irishman, who had leaped straight for the sled in a desperate attempt to capture it; but he was an instant too late. Striking on the very rear of it, he was thrown from his feet, backward, into the snow. Yet, with the quickness of a cat, he had clutched the end of the sled with one hand, turned over, and was dragging behind on his breast, swearing at the boy and threatening all kinds of terrible things if he did not stop the dogs; but Walt cracked him sharply across the knuckles with the butt of the dog whip till he let go.

It was eight miles from Walt's claim to the Yukon—eight very crooked miles, for the creek wound back and forth like a snake, "tying knots in itself," as George Lukens said. And because it was so crooked the dogs could not get up their best speed, while the sled ground heavily on its side against the curves, now to the right, now to the left.

Travelers who had come up and down the Mazy May on foot, with packs on their backs, had declined to go round all the bends, and instead had made shortcuts across the narrow necks of creek bottom. Two of his pursuers had gone back to harness the remaining dogs, but the others took advantage of these shortcuts, running on foot, and before he knew it they had almost overtaken him.

"Halt!" they cried after him. "Stop, or we'll shoot!"

But Walt only yelled the harder at the dogs, and dashed around the bend with a couple of revolver bullets singing after him. At the next bend they had drawn up closer still, and the bullets struck uncomfortably near him but at this point the Mazy May straightened out and ran for half a mile as the crow flies. Here the dogs stretched out in their long wolf swing, and the stampeders, quickly winded, slowed down and waited for their own sled to come up.

Looking over his shoulder, Walt reasoned that they had not given up the chase for good, and that they would soon be after him again. So he wrapped the fur robe about him to shut out the stinging air, and lay flat on the empty sled, encouraging the dogs, as he well knew how.

At last, twisting abruptly between two river islands, he came upon the mighty Yukon sweeping grandly to the north. He could not see from bank to bank, and in the quick-falling twilight it loomed a great white sea of frozen stillness. There was not a sound, save the breathing of the dogs, and the churn of the steel-shod sled.

No snow had fallen for several weeks, and the traffic had packed the main river trail till it was hard and glassy as glare ice. Over this the sled flew along, and the dogs kept the trail fairly well, although Walt quickly discovered that he had made a mistake in choosing the leader. As they were driven in single file, without reins, he had to guide them by his voice, and it was evident the head dog had never learned the meaning of "gee" and "haw." He hugged the inside of the curves too closely, often forcing his comrades behind him into the soft snow, while several times he thus capsized the sled.

There was no wind, but the speed at which he traveled created a bitter blast, and with the thermometer down to forty below, this bit through fur and flesh to the very bones. Aware that if he remained constantly upon the sled he would freeze to death, and knowing the practice of Arctic travelers, Walt shortened up one of the lashing thongs, and whenever he felt chilled, seized hold of it, jumped off, and ran behind till warmth was restored. Then he would climb on and rest till the process had to be repeated.

Looking back he could see the sled of his pursuers, drawn by eight dogs, rising and falling over the ice hummocks like a boat in a seaway. The Irishman and the black-bearded leader were with it, taking turns in running and riding.

TAKE NOTES

TAKE NOTES

Night fell, and in the blackness of the first hour or so Walt toiled desperately with his dogs. On account of the poor lead dog, they were continually floundering off the beaten track into the soft snow, and the sled was as often riding on its side or top as it was in the proper way. This work and strain tried his strength sorely. Had he not been in such haste he could have avoided much of it, but he feared the stampeders would creep up in the darkness and overtake him. However, he could hear them yelling to their dogs, and knew from the sounds they were coming up very slowly.

When the moon rose he was off Sixty Mile, and Dawson was only fifty miles away. He was almost exhausted, and breathed a sigh of relief as he climbed on the sled again. Looking back, he saw his enemies had crawled up within four hundred yards. At this space they remained, a black speck of motion on the white river breast. Strive as they would, they could not shorten this distance, and strive as he would, he could not increase it.

Walt had now discovered the proper lead dog, and he knew he could easily run away from them if he could only change the bad leader for the good one. But this was impossible, for a moment's delay, at the speed they were running, would bring the men behind upon him.

When he was off the mouth of Rosebud Creek, just as he was topping a rise, the report of a gun and the ping of a bullet on the ice beside him told him that they were this time shooting at him with a rifle. And from then on, as he cleared the summit of each ice jam, he stretched flat on the leaping sled till the rifle shot from the rear warned him that he was safe till the next ice jam was reached.

Now it is very hard to lie on a moving sled, jumping and plunging and yawing[4] like a boat before the wind, and to shoot through the deceiving moonlight at an object four hundred yards away on another moving sled performing equally wild antics. So it is not to be wondered at that the black-bearded leader did not hit him.

---

4. **yawing** (yôʹ iŋ) *adj.* swinging from side to side.

After several hours of this, during which, perhaps, a score of bullets had struck about him, their ammunition began to give out and their fire slackened. They took greater care, and shot at him at the most favorable opportunities. He was also leaving them behind, the distance slowly increasing to six hundred yards.

Lifting clear on the crest of a great jam off Indian River, Walt Masters met with his first accident. A bullet sang past his ears, and struck the bad lead dog.

The poor brute plunged in a heap, with the rest of the team on top of him.

Like a flash Walt was by the leader. Cutting the traces with his hunting knife, he dragged the dying animal to one side and straightened out the team.

He glanced back. The other sled was coming up like an express train. With half the dogs still over their traces, he cried "Mush on!" and leaped upon the sled just as the pursuers dashed abreast[5] of him.

The Irishman was preparing to spring for him—they were so sure they had him that they did not shoot—when Walt turned fiercely upon them with his whip.

He struck at their faces, and men must save their faces with their hands. So there was no shooting just then. Before they could recover from the hot rain of blows, Walt reached out from his sled, catching their wheel dog by the forelegs in midspring, and throwing him heavily. This snarled the team, capsizing the sled and tangling his enemies up beautifully.

Away Walt flew, the runners of his sled fairly screaming as they bounded over the frozen surface. And what had seemed an accident proved to be a blessing in disguise. The proper lead dog was now to the fore, and he stretched low and whined with joy as he jerked his comrades along.

By the time he reached Ainslie's Creek, seventeen miles from Dawson, Walt had left his pursuers, a tiny speck, far behind. At Monte Cristo Island he could no longer see them. And at Swede Creek, just as daylight was silvering the pines, he ran plump into the camp of old Loren Hall.

TAKE NOTES

---

5. abreast (ə brest′) *adv.* alongside.

TAKE NOTES

Almost as quick as it takes to tell it, Loren had his sleeping furs rolled up, and had joined Walt on the sled. They permitted the dogs to travel more slowly, as there was no sign of the chase in the rear, and just as they pulled up at the gold commissioner's office in Dawson, Walt, who had kept his eyes open to the last, fell asleep.

And because of what Walt Masters did on this night, the men of the Yukon have become proud of him, and speak of him now as the King of Mazy May.

from Zlata's Diary

by Zlata Filipović

TAKE NOTES

Monday, March 30, 1992

Hey, Diary! You know what I think? Since Anne Frank[1] called her diary Kitty, maybe I could give you a name too. What about:

ASFALTINA PIDZAMETA
SEFIKA HIKMETA
SEVALA MIMMY

or something else???

I'm thinking, thinking . . .

I've decided! I'm going to call you

MIMMY

All right, then, let's start.

Dear Mimmy,
It's almost half-term. We're all studying for our tests. Tomorrow we're supposed to go to a classical music concert at the Skenderija Hall. Our teacher says we shouldn't go because there will be 10,000 people, pardon me, children, there, and somebody might take us as hostages or plant a bomb in the concert hall. Mommy says I shouldn't go. So I won't.

Hey! You know who won the Yugovision Song Contest?! EXTRA NENA!!!???

I'm afraid to say this next thing. Melica says she heard at the hairdresser's that on Saturday, April 4, 1992, there's going to be BOOM—BOOM, BANG—BANG, CRASH Sarajevo. Translation: they're going to bomb Sarajevo.

Love,
Zlata

1. **Anne Frank** In 1942, 13-year-old Anne Frank began a diary that she kept for the two years she and her family and some others hid from the Nazis in an attic in Amsterdam. Anne died in a concentration camp in 1945. Her father published parts of the diary in 1947, and it has since become a classic.

TAKE NOTES

Sunday, April 12, 1992

Dear Mimmy,
The new sections of town—Dobrinja, Mojmilo, Vojnicko polje—are being badly shelled. Everything is being destroyed, burned, the people are in shelters. Here in the middle of town, where we live, it's different. It's quiet.

People go out. It was a nice warm spring day today. We went out too. Vaso Miskin Street was full of people, children. It looked like a peace march. People came out to be together, they don't want war. They want to live and enjoy themselves the way they used to. That's only natural, isn't it? Who likes or wants war, when it's the worst thing in the world?

I keep thinking about the march I joined today. It's bigger and stronger than war. That's why it will win. The people must be the ones to win, not the war, because war has nothing to do with humanity. War is something inhuman.

Zlata

Tuesday, April 14, 1992

Dear Mimmy,
People are leaving Sarajevo. The airport, train and bus stations are packed. I saw sad pictures on TV of people parting. Families, friends separating. Some are leaving, others staying. It's so sad. Why? These people and children aren't guilty of anything. Keka and Braco[2] came early this morning. They're in the kitchen with Mommy and Daddy, whispering. Keka and Mommy are crying. I don't think they know what to do—whether to stay or to go. Neither way is good.

Zlata

Saturday, May 2, 1992

Dear Mimmy,
Today was truly, absolutely the worst day ever in Sarajevo. The shooting started around noon. Mommy

2. **Keka and Braco** nicknames of a husband and wife who are friends of Zlata's parents.

and I moved into the hall. Daddy was in his office, under our apartment, at the time. We told him on the intercom to run quickly to the downstairs lobby where we'd meet him. We brought Cicko[3] with us. The gunfire was getting worse, and we couldn't get over the wall to the Bobars',[4] so we ran down to our own cellar.

The cellar is ugly, dark, smelly. Mommy, who's terrified of mice, had two fears to cope with. The three of us were in the same corner as the other day. We listened to the pounding shells, the shooting, the thundering noise overhead. We even heard planes. At one moment I realized that this awful cellar was the only place that could save our lives. Suddenly, it started to look almost warm and nice. It was the only way we could defend ourselves against all this terrible shooting. We heard glass shattering in our street. Horrible. I put my fingers in my ears to block out the terrible sounds. I was worried about Cicko. We had left him behind in the lobby. Would he catch cold there? Would something hit him? I was terribly hungry and thirsty. We had left our half-cooked lunch in the kitchen.

When the shooting died down a bit, Daddy ran over to our apartment and brought us back some sandwiches. He said he could smell something burning and that the phones weren't working. He brought our TV set down to the cellar. That's when we learned that the main post office (near us) was on fire and that they had kidnapped our President. At around 8:00 we went back up to our apartment. Almost every window in our street was broken. Ours were all right, thank God. I saw the post office in flames. A terrible sight. The fire-fighters battled with the raging fire. Daddy took a few photos of the post office being devoured by the flames. He said they wouldn't come out because I had been fiddling with something on the camera. I was sorry. The whole apartment smelled of the burning fire. God, and I used to pass by there every day. It had just been done up. It was huge and beautiful, and now it was being swallowed up by the flames. It was disappearing. That's what this neighborhood of mine looks like, my Mimmy.

TAKE NOTES

---

3. **Cicko** (chēk´ ō) Zlata's canary.
4. **Bobars'** (Bō´ bërs) next-door neighbors.

TAKE NOTES

I wonder what it's like in other parts of town? I heard on the radio that it was awful around the Eternal Flame.[5] The place is knee-deep in glass. We're worried about Grandma and Granddad. They live there. Tomorrow, if we can go out, we'll see how they are. A terrible day. This has been the worst, most awful day in my eleven-year-old life. I hope it will be the only one. Mommy and Daddy are very edgy. I have to go to bed.

Ciao![6]
Zlata

Tuesday, May 5, 1992

Dear Mimmy,
The shooting seems to be dying down. I guess they've caused enough misery, although I don't know why. It has something to do with politics. I just hope the "kids" come to some agreement. Oh, if only they would, so we could live and breathe as human beings again. The things that have happened here these past few days are terrible. I want it to stop forever. PEACE! PEACE!

I didn't tell you, Mimmy, that we've rearranged things in the apartment. My room and Mommy and Daddy's are too dangerous to be in. They face the hills, which is where they're shooting from. If only you knew how scared I am to go near the windows and into those rooms. So, we turned a safe corner of the sitting room into a "bedroom." We sleep on mattresses on the floor. It's strange and awful. But, it's safer that way. We've turned everything around for safety. We put Cicko in the kitchen. He's safe there, although once the shooting starts there's nowhere safe except the cellar. I suppose all this will stop and we'll all go back to our usual places.

Ciao!
Zlata

5. **Eternal Flame** Sarajevo landmark that honors those who died resisting the Nazi occupation during World War II.
6. **Ciao!** (chou) *interj.* hello or goodbye.

Thursday, May 7, 1992

Dear Mimmy,
I was almost positive the war would stop, but today . . . Today a shell fell on the park in front of my house, the park where I used to play and sit with my girlfriends. A lot of people were hurt. From what I hear Jaca, Jaca's mother, Selma, Nina, our neighbor Dado and who knows how many other people who happened to be there were wounded. Dado, Jaca and her mother have come home from the hospital, Selma lost a kidney but I don't know how she is, because she's still in the hospital. AND NINA IS DEAD. A piece of shrapnel lodged in her brain and she died. She was such a sweet, nice little girl. We went to kindergarten together, and we used to play together in the park. Is it possible I'll never see Nina again? Nina, an innocent eleven-year-old little girl—the victim of a stupid war. I feel sad. I cry and wonder why? She didn't do anything. A disgusting war has destroyed a young child's life. Nina. I'll always remember you as a wonderful little girl.

Love, Mimmy,
Zlata

Monday, June 29, 1992

Dear Mimmy,
BOREDOM!!! SHOOTING!!! SHELLING!!! PEOPLE BEING KILLED!!! DESPAIR!!! HUNGER!!! MISERY!!! FEAR!!!

That's my life! The life of an innocent eleven-year-old schoolgirl!! A schoolgirl without a school, without the fun and excitement of school. A child without games, without friends, without the sun, without birds, without nature, without fruit, without chocolate or sweets, with just a little powdered milk. In short, a child without a childhood. A wartime child. I now realize that I am really living through a war, I am witnessing an ugly, disgusting war. I and thousands of other children in this town that is being destroyed, that is crying, weeping, seeking help, but getting none. God, will this ever stop, will I ever be a schoolgirl again,

TAKE NOTES

TAKE NOTES

will I ever enjoy my childhood again? I once heard that childhood is the most wonderful time of your life. And it is. I loved it, and now an ugly war is taking it all away from me. Why? I feel sad. I feel like crying. I am crying.

Your Zlata

Thursday, October 29, 1992

Dear Mimmy,

Mommy and Auntie Ivanka (from her office) have received grants to specialize in Holland. They have letters of guarantee,[7] and there's even one for me. But Mommy can't decide. If she accepts, she leaves behind Daddy, her parents, her brother. I think it's a hard decision to make. One minute I think—no, I'm against it. But then I remember the war, winter, hunger, my stolen childhood and I feel like going. Then I think of Daddy, Grandma and Granddad, and I don't want to go. It's hard to know what to do. I'm really on edge, Mimmy, I can't write anymore.

Your Zlata

Monday, November 2, 1992

Dear Mimmy,

Mommy thought it over, talked to Daddy, Grandma and Granddad, and to me, and she's decided to go. The reason for her decision is—ME. What's happening in Sarajevo is already too much for me, and the coming winter will make it even harder. All right. But . . . well, I suppose it's better for me to go. I really can't stand it here anymore. I talked to Auntie Ivanka today and she told me that this war is hardest on the children, and that the children should be got out of the city. Daddy will manage, maybe he'll even get to come with us.

Ciao!
Zlata

7. **letters of guarantee** letters from people or companies promising to help individuals who wanted to leave the country during the war.

Thursday, December 3, 1992

Dear Mimmy,
Today is my birthday. My first wartime birthday. Twelve years old. Congratulations. Happy birthday to me!

The day started off with kisses and congratulations. First Mommy and Daddy, then everyone else. Mommy and Daddy gave me three Chinese vanity cases—with flowers on them!

As usual there was no electricity. Auntie Melica came with her family (Kenan, Naida, Nihad) and gave me a book. And Braco Lajtner came, of course. The whole neighborhood got together in the evening. I got chocolate, vitamins, a heart-shaped soap (small, orange), a key chain with a picture of Maja and Bojana, a pendant made of a stone from Cyprus, a ring (silver) and earrings (bingo!).

The table was nicely laid, with little rolls, fish and rice salad, cream cheese (with Feta), canned corned beef, a pie, and, of course—a birthday cake. Not how it used to be, but there's a war on. Luckily there was no shooting, so we could celebrate.

It was nice, but something was missing. It's called peace!

Your Zlata

Tuesday, July 27, 1993

Dear Mimmy,

Journalists, reporters, TV and radio crews from all over the world (even Japan). They're interested in you, Mimmy, and ask me about you, but also about me. It's exciting. Nice. Unusual for a wartime child.

My days have changed a little. They're more interesting now. It takes my mind off things. When I go to bed at night I think about the day behind me. Nice, as though it weren't wartime, and with such thoughts I happily fall asleep.

TAKE NOTES

TAKE NOTES

But in the morning, when the wheels of the water carts wake me up, I realize that there's a war on, that mine is a wartime life. SHOOTING, NO ELECTRICITY, NO WATER, NO GAS, NO FOOD. Almost no life.

Zlata

Thursday, October 7, 1993

Dear Mimmy,
Things are the way they used to be, lately. There's no shooting (thank God), I go to school, read, play the piano . . .

Winter is approaching, but we have nothing to heat with.

I look at the calendar and it seems as though this year of 1993 will again be marked by war. God, we've lost two years listening to gunfire, battling with electricity, water, food, and waiting for peace.

I look at Mommy and Daddy. In two years they've aged ten. And me? I haven't aged, but I've grown, although I honestly don't know how. I don't eat fruit or vegetables, I don't drink juices, I don't eat meat . . . I am a child of rice, peas and spaghetti. There I am talking about food again. I often catch myself dreaming about chicken, a good cutlet, pizza, lasagna . . . Oh, enough of that.

Zlata

Tuesday, October 12, 1993

Dear Mimmy,
I don't remember whether I told you that last summer I sent a letter through school to a pen-pal in America. It was a letter for an American girl or boy.

Today I got an answer. A boy wrote to me. His name is Brandon, he's twelve like me, and lives in Harrisburg, Pennsylvania. It really made me happy.

I don't know who invented the mail and letters, but thank you whoever you are. I now have a friend in America, and Brandon has a friend in Sarajevo. This is my first letter from across the Atlantic. And in it is a reply envelope, and a lovely pencil.

A Canadian TV crew and journalist from *The Sunday Times* (Janine) came to our gym class today. They brought me two chocolate bars. What a treat. It's been a long time since I've had sweets.

Love,
Zlata

December 1993

Dear Mimmy,

PARIS. There's electricity, there's water, there's gas. There's, there's . . . life, Mimmy. Yes, life; bright lights, traffic, people, food . . . Don't think I've gone nuts, Mimmy. Hey, listen to me, Paris!? No, I'm not crazy, I'm not kidding, it really is Paris and (can you believe it?) me in it. Me, my Mommy and my Daddy. At last. You're 100% sure I'm crazy, but I'm serious, I'm telling you, dear Mimmy, that I have arrived in Paris. I've come to be with you. You're mine again now and together we're moving into the light. The darkness has played out its part. The darkness is behind us; now we're bathed in light lit by good people. Remember that—good people. Bulb by bulb, not candles, but bulb by bulb, and me bathing in the lights of Paris. Yes, Paris. Incredible. You don't understand. You know, I don't think I understand either. I feel as though I must be crazy, dreaming, as though it's a fairy tale, but it's all TRUE.

TAKE NOTES

TAKE NOTES

The Drive-In Movies

by Gary Soto

For our family, moviegoing was rare. But if our mom, tired from a week of candling eggs,[1] woke up happy on a Saturday morning, there was a chance we might later scramble to our blue Chevy and beat nightfall to the Starlight Drive-In. My brother and sister knew this. I knew this. So on Saturday we tried to be good. We sat in the cool shadows of the TV with the volume low and watched cartoons, a prelude of what was to come.

One Saturday I decided to be extra good. When she came out of the bedroom tying her robe, she yawned a hat-sized yawn and blinked red eyes at the weak brew of coffee I had fixed for her. I made her toast with strawberry jam spread to all the corners and set the three boxes of cereal in front of her. If she didn't care to eat cereal, she could always look at the back of the boxes as she drank her coffee.

I went outside. The lawn was tall but too wet with dew to mow. I picked up a trowel[2] and began to weed the flower bed. The weeds were really bermuda grass, long stringers that ran finger-deep in the ground. I got to work quickly and in no time crescents of earth began rising under my fingernails. I was sweaty hot. My knees hurt from kneeling, and my brain was dull from making the trowel go up and down, dribbling crumbs of earth. I dug for half an hour, then stopped to play with the neighbor's dog and pop ticks from his poor snout.

I then mowed the lawn, which was still beaded with dew and noisy with bees hovering over clover. This job was less dull because as I pushed the mower over the shaggy lawn, I could see it looked tidier. My brother and sister watched from the window. Their faces were fat with cereal, a third helping. I made a face at

1. **candling eggs** examining uncooked eggs for freshness by placing them in front of a burning candle.
2. **trowel** (trou´ əl) *n.* a small hand tool used by gardeners to weed or dig.

them when they asked how come I was working. Rick pointed to part of the lawn. "You missed some over there." I ignored him and kept my attention on the windmill of grassy blades. •

While I was emptying the catcher, a bee stung the bottom of my foot. I danced on one leg and was ready to cry when Mother showed her face at the window. I sat down on the grass and examined my foot: the stinger was pulsating. I pulled it out quickly, ran water over the sting and packed it with mud, Grandmother's remedy.

Hobbling, I returned to the flower bed where I pulled more stringers and again played with the dog. More ticks had migrated to his snout. I swept the front steps, took out the garbage, cleaned the lint filter to the dryer (easy), plucked hair from the industrial wash basin in the garage (also easy), hosed off the patio, smashed three snails sucking paint from the house (disgusting but fun), tied a bundle of newspapers, put away toys, and, finally, seeing that almost everything was done and the sun was not too high, started waxing the car.

My brother joined me with an old gym sock, and our sister watched us while sucking on a cherry Kool-Aid ice cube. The liquid wax drooled onto the sock, and we began to swirl the white slop on the chrome. My arms ached from buffing, which though less boring than weeding, was harder. But the beauty was evident. The shine, hurting our eyes and glinting like an armful of dimes, brought Mother out. She looked around the yard and said, "Pretty good." She winced at the grille and returned inside the house.

We began to wax the paint. My brother applied the liquid and I followed him rubbing hard in wide circles as we moved around the car. I began to hurry because my arms were hurting and my stung foot looked like a water balloon. We were working around the trunk when Rick pounded on the bottle of wax. He squeezed the bottle and it sneezed a few more white drops.

We looked at each other. "There's some on the sock," I said. "Let's keep going." •

We polished and buffed, sweat weeping on our brows. We got scared when we noticed that the gym sock was now blue. The paint was coming off. Our

TAKE NOTES

TAKE NOTES

sister fit ice cubes into our mouths and we worked harder, more intently, more dedicated to the car and our mother. We ran the sock over the chrome, trying to pick up extra wax. But there wasn't enough to cover the entire car. Only half got waxed, but we thought it was better than nothing and went inside for lunch. After lunch, we returned outside with tasty sandwiches.

Rick and I nearly jumped. The waxed side of the car was foggy white. We took a rag and began to polish vigorously and nearly in tears, but the fog wouldn't come off. I blamed Rick and he blamed me. Debra stood at the window, not wanting to get involved. Now, not only would we not go to the movies, but Mom would surely snap a branch from the plum tree and chase us around the yard.

Mom came out and looked at us with hands on her aproned hips. Finally, she said, "You boys worked so hard." She turned on the garden hose and washed the car. That night we did go to the drive-in. The first feature was about nothing, and the second feature, starring Jerry Lewis, was *Cinderfella*. I tried to stay awake. I kept a wad of homemade popcorn in my cheek and laughed when Jerry Lewis fit golf tees in his nose. I rubbed my watery eyes. I laughed and looked at my mom. I promised myself I would remember that scene with the golf tees and promised myself not to work so hard the coming Saturday. Twenty minutes into the movie, I fell asleep with one hand in the popcorn.

Langston Terrace

by Eloise Greenfield

TAKE NOTES

I fell in love with Langston Terrace the very first time I saw it. Our family had been living in two rooms of a three-story house when Mama and Daddy saw the newspaper article telling of the plans to build it. It was going to be a low-rent housing project in northeast Washington, and it would be named in honor of John Mercer Langston, the famous black lawyer, educator, and congressman.

So many people needed housing and wanted to live there, many more than there would be room for. They were all filling out applications, hoping to be one of the 274 families chosen. My parents filled out one, too.

I didn't want to move. I knew our house was crowded—there were eleven of us, six adults and five children—but I didn't want to leave my friends, and I didn't want to go to a strange place and be the new person in a neighborhood and a school where most of the other children already knew each other. I was eight years old, and I had been to three schools. We had moved five times since we'd been in Washington, each time trying to get more space and a better place to live. But rent was high so we'd always lived in a house with relatives and friends, and shared the rent. •

One of the people in our big household was Lillie, Daddy's cousin and Mama's best friend. She and her husband also applied for a place in the new project, and during the months that it was being built, Lillie and Mama would sometimes walk fifteen blocks just to stand and watch the workmen digging holes and laying bricks. They'd just stand there watching and wishing. And at home, that was all they could talk about. "When we get our new placc . . ." "If we get our new place . . ."

Lillie got her good news first. I can still see her and Mama standing at the bottom of the hall steps, hugging and laughing and crying, happy for Lillie, then sitting on the steps, worrying and wishing again for Mama.

TAKE NOTES

Finally, one evening, a woman came to the house with our good news, and Mama and Daddy went over and picked out the house they wanted. We moved on my ninth birthday. Wilbur, Gerald, and I went to school that morning from one house, and when Daddy came to pick us up, he took us home to another one. All the furniture had been moved while we were in school. •

Langston Terrace was a lovely birthday present. It was built on a hill, a group of tan brick houses and apartments with a playground as its center. The red mud surrounding the concrete walks had not yet been covered with black soil and grass seed, and the holes that would soon be homes for young trees were filled with rainwater. But it still looked beautiful to me.

We had a whole house all to ourselves. Upstairs and downstairs. Two bedrooms, and the living room would be my bedroom at night. Best of all, I wasn't the only new person. Everybody was new to this new little community, and by the time school opened in the fall, we had gotten used to each other and had made friends with other children in the neighborhood, too. •

I guess most of the parents thought of the new place as an in-between place. They were glad to be there, but their dream was to save enough money to pay for a house that would be their own. Saving was hard, though, and slow, because each time somebody in a family got a raise on the job, it had to be reported to the manager of the project so that the rent could be raised, too. Most people stayed years longer than they had planned to, but they didn't let that stop them from enjoying life.

They formed a resident council to look into any neighborhood problems that might come up. They started a choral group and presented music and poetry programs on Sunday evenings in the social room or on the playground. On weekends, they played horseshoes and softball and other games. They had a reading club that met once a week at the Langston branch of the public library, after it opened in the basement of one of the apartment buildings.

The library was very close to my house. I could leave by my back door and be there in two minutes. The playground was right in front of my house, and after my sister Vedie was born and we moved a few doors down to a three-bedroom house, I could just look out of my bedroom window to see if any of my friends were out playing.

There were so many games to play and things to do. We played hide-and-seek at the lamppost, paddle tennis and shuffleboard, dodge ball and jacks. We danced in fireplug showers, jumped rope to rhymes, played "Bouncy, Bouncy, Bally," swinging one leg over a bouncing ball, played baseball on a nearby field, had parties in the social room and bus trips to the beach. In the playroom, we played Ping-Pong and pool, learned to sew and embroider and crochet.

For us, Langston Terrace wasn't an in-between place. It was a growing-up place, a good growing-up place. Neighbors who cared, family and friends, and a lot of fun. Life was good. Not perfect, but good. We knew about problems, heard about them, saw them, lived through some hard ones ourselves, but our community wrapped itself around us, put itself between us and the hard knocks, to cushion the blows. •

It's been many years since I moved away, but every once in a long while I go back, just to look at things and remember. The large stone animals that decorated the playground are still there. A walrus, a hippo, a frog, and two horses. They've started to crack now, but I remember when they first came to live with us. They were friends, to climb on or to lean against, or to gather around in the evening. You could sit on the frog's head and look way out over the city at the tall trees and rooftops.

Nowadays, whenever I run into old friends, mostly at a funeral, or maybe a wedding, after we've talked about how we've been and what we've been doing, and how old our children are, we always end up talking about our childtime in our old neighborhood. And somebody will say, "One of these days we ought to have a Langston reunion." That's what we always called it, just "Langston," without the "Terrace." I guess because it sounded more homey. And that's what Langston was. It was home.

TAKE NOTES

TAKE NOTES

Jackie Robinson: Justice at Last

by Geoffrey C. Ward and Ken Burns

It was 1945, and World War II had ended. Americans of all races had died for their country. Yet black men were still not allowed in the major leagues. The national pastime was loved by all America, but the major leagues were for white men only.

Branch Rickey of the Brooklyn Dodgers thought that was wrong. He was the only team owner who believed blacks and whites should play together. Baseball, he felt, would become even more thrilling, and fans of all colors would swarm to his ballpark.

Rickey decided his team would be the first to integrate. There were plenty of brilliant Negro league players, but he knew the first black major leaguer would need much more than athletic ability.

Many fans and players were prejudiced—they didn't want the races to play together. Rickey knew the first black player would be cursed and booed. Pitchers would throw at him; runners would spike him. Even his own teammates might try to pick a fight.

But somehow this man had to rise above that. No matter what happened, he must never lose his temper. No matter what was said to him, he must never answer back. If he had even one fight, people might say integration wouldn't work.

When Rickey met Jackie Robinson, he thought he'd found the right man. Robinson was 28 years old, and a superb athlete. In his first season in the Negro leagues, he hit .387. But just as importantly, he had great intelligence and sensitivity. Robinson was college-educated, and knew what joining the majors would mean for blacks. The grandson of a slave, he was proud of his race and wanted others to feel the same.

In the past, Robinson had always stood up for his rights. But now Rickey told him he would have to stop. The Dodgers needed "a man that will take abuse."

At first Robinson thought Rickey wanted someone who was afraid to defend himself. But as they talked, he realized that in this case a truly brave man would have to avoid fighting. He thought for a while, then promised Rickey he would not fight back.

Robinson signed with the Dodgers and went to play in the minors in 1946. Rickey was right—fans insulted him, and so did players. But he performed brilliantly and avoided fights. Then, in 1947, he came to the majors.

Many Dodgers were angry. Some signed a petition demanding to be traded. But Robinson and Rickey were determined to make their experiment work.

On April 15—Opening Day—26,623 fans came out to Ebbets Field. More than half of them were black—Robinson was already their hero. Now he was making history just by being on the field.

The afternoon was cold and wet, but no one left the ballpark. The Dodgers beat the Boston Braves, 5–3. Robinson went hitless, but the hometown fans didn't seem to care—they cheered his every move.

Robinson's first season was difficult. Fans threatened to kill him; players tried to hurt him. The St. Louis Cardinals said they would strike if he took the field. And because of laws separating the races in certain states, he often couldn't eat or sleep in the same places as his teammates.

Yet through it all, he kept his promise to Rickey. No matter who insulted him, he never retaliated.

Robinson's dignity paid off. Thousands of fans jammed stadiums to see him play. The Dodgers set attendance records in a number of cities.

Slowly his teammates accepted him, realizing that he was the spark that made them a winning team. No one was more daring on the base paths or better with the glove. At the plate, he had great bat control—he could hit the ball anywhere. That season, he was named baseball's first Rookie of the Year.

Jackie Robinson went on to a glorious career. But he did more than play the game well—his bravery taught Americans a lesson. Branch Rickey opened a door, and Jackie Robinson stepped through it, making sure it could never be closed again. Something wonderful happened to baseball—and America—the day Jackie Robinson joined the Dodgers.

TAKE NOTES

TAKE NOTES

Oranges

by Gary Soto

The first time I walked
With a girl, I was twelve,
Cold, and weighted down
With two oranges in my jacket.
December. Frost cracking
Beneath my steps, my breath
Before me, then gone,
As I walked toward
Her house, the one whose
Porch light burned yellow
Night and day, in any weather.
A dog barked at me, until
She came out pulling
At her gloves, face bright
With rouge[1]. I smiled,
Touched her shoulder, and led
Her down the street, across
A used car lot and a line
Of newly planted trees,
Until we were breathing
Before a drugstore. We
Entered, the tiny bell
Bringing a saleslady
Down a narrow aisle of goods.
I turned to the candies
Tiered[2] like bleachers,
And asked what she wanted—
Light in her eyes, a smile
Starting at the corners
Of her mouth. I fingered
A nickel in my pocket,

1. **rouge** (ro͞ozh) *n.* a reddish cosmetic used to color the cheeks.
2. **tiered** (tird) *adj.* arranged in levels, one above another.

And when she lifted a chocolate
That cost a dime,
I didn't say anything.
I took the nickel from
My pocket, then an orange,
And set them quietly on
The counter. When I looked up,
The lady's eyes met mine,
And held them, knowing
Very well what it was all
About.
    Outside,
A few cars hissing past,
Fog hanging like old
Coats between the trees.
I took my girl's hand
In mine for two blocks,
Then released it to let
Her unwrap the chocolate.
I peeled my orange
That was so bright against
The gray of December
That, from some distance,
Someone might have thought
I was making a fire in my hands.

TAKE NOTES

TAKE NOTES

Ode to Family Photographs

by Gary Soto

This is the pond, and these are my feet.
This is the rooster, and this is more of my feet.

Mamá was never good at pictures.

This is a statue of a famous general who lost an arm
And this is me with my head cut off.

This is a trash can chained to a gate,
This is my father with his eyes half-closed.

This is a photograph of my sister
And a giraffe looking over her shoulder.

This is our car's front bumper.
This is a bird with a pretzel in its beak.
This is my brother Pedro standing on one leg on a rock,
With a smear of chocolate on his face.

Mamá sneezed when she looked
Behind the camera: the snapshots are blurry,
The angles dizzy as a spin on a merry-go-round.

But we had fun when Mamá picked up the camera.
How can I tell?
Each of us laughing hard.
Can you see? I have candy in my mouth.

A Dream Within a Dream

by Edgar Allan Poe

TAKE NOTES

Take this kiss upon the brow!
And, in parting from you now,
Thus much let me avow—
You are not wrong, who deem
That my days have been a dream;
Yet if hope has flown away
In a night, or in a day,
In a vision, or in none,
Is it therefore the less *gone*?
All that we see or seem
Is but a dream within a dream.
I stand amid the roar
Of a surf-tormented shore,
And I hold within my hand
Grains of the golden sand—
How few! yet how they creep
Through my fingers to the deep,
While I weep—while I weep!
O God! can I not grasp
Them with a tighter clasp?
O God! can I not save
One from the pitiless wave?
Is *all* that we see or seem
But a dream within a dream?

TAKE NOTES

Adventures of Isabel

by Ogden Nash

Isabel met an enormous bear,
Isabel, Isabel, didn't care;
The bear was hungry, the bear was ravenous,
The bear's big mouth was cruel and cavernous.
The bear said, Isabel, glad to meet you,
How do, Isabel, now I'll eat you!
Isabel, Isabel, didn't worry,
Isabel didn't scream or scurry.
She washed her hands and
she straightened her hair up,
Then Isabel quietly ate the bear up.

Once in a night as black as pitch
Isabel met a wicked old witch.
The witch's face was cross and wrinkled,
The witch's gums with teeth were sprinkled.
Ho ho, Isabel! the old witch crowed,
I'll turn you into an ugly toad!
Isabel, Isabel, didn't worry,
Isabel didn't scream or scurry,
She showed no rage and she showed no rancor,
But she turned the witch into milk and drank her.

Isabel met a hideous giant,
Isabel continued self-reliant.
The giant was hairy, the giant was horrid,
He had one eye in the middle of his forehead.
Good morning Isabel, the giant said,
I'll grind your bones to make my bread.
Isabel, Isabel, didn't worry,
Isabel didn't scream or scurry.
She nibbled the zwieback that she always fed off,
And when it was gone, she cut the giant's head off.

Isabel met a troublesome doctor,
He punched and he poked till he really shocked
her.

The doctor's talk was of coughs and chills
And the doctor's satchel bulged with pills.
The doctor said unto Isabel,
Swallow this, it will make you well.
Isabel, Isabel, didn't worry,
Isabel didn't scream or scurry.
She took those pills from the pill concocter,
And Isabel calmly cured the doctor.

TAKE NOTES

TAKE NOTES

Life Doesn't Frighten Me

by Maya Angelou

Shadows on the wall
Noises down the hall
Life doesn't frighten me at all
Bad dogs barking loud
Big ghosts in a cloud
Life doesn't frighten me at all.

Mean old Mother Goose
Lions on the loose
They don't frighten me at all
Dragons breathing flame
On my counterpane[1]
That doesn't frighten me at all.

I go boo
Make them shoo
I make fun
Way they run
I won't cry
So they fly
I just smile
They go wild
Life doesn't frighten me at all.

Tough guys in a fight
All alone at night
Life doesn't frighten me at all.

Panthers in the park
Strangers in the dark
No, they don't frighten me at all.

That new classroom where
Boys all pull my hair
(Kissy little girls
With their hair in curls)
They don't frighten me at all.

1. **counterpane** *n.* bedspread.

Don't show me frogs and snakes
And listen for my scream,
If I'm afraid at all
It's only in my dreams.

I've got a magic charm
That I keep up my sleeve,
I can walk the ocean floor
And never have to breathe.

Life doesn't frighten me at all
Not at all
Not at all.
Life doesn't frighten me at all.

TAKE NOTES

TAKE NOTES

The Walrus and the Carpenter

by Lewis Carroll

The sun was shining on the sea,
Shining with all his might:
He did his very best to make
The billows smooth and bright—
And this was odd, because it was
The middle of the night.

The moon was shining sulkily,
Because she thought the sun
Had got no business to be there
After the day was done—
"It's very rude of him," she said,
"To come and spoil the fun!"

The sea was wet as wet could be,
The sands were dry as dry.
You could not see a cloud, because
No cloud was in the sky:
No birds were flying overhead—
There were no birds to fly.

The Walrus and the Carpenter
Were walking close at hand:
They wept like anything to see
Such quantities of sand:
"If this were only cleared away,"
They said, "it would be grand!"

"If seven maids with seven mops
Swept it for half a year,
Do you suppose," the Walrus said,
"That they could get it clear?"
"I doubt it," said the Carpenter,
And shed a bitter tear.

"O Oysters, come and walk with us!"
The Walrus did beseech.

"A pleasant walk, a pleasant talk,
  Along the briny beach:
We cannot do with more than four,
  To give a hand to each."

The eldest Oyster looked at him,
  But never a word he said:
The eldest Oyster winked his eye,
  And shook his heavy head—
Meaning to say he did not choose
  To leave the oyster-bed.

But four young Oysters hurried up,
  All eager for this treat:
Their coats were brushed, their faces washed,
  Their shoes were clean and neat—
And this was odd, because, you know,
  They hadn't any feet.

Four other Oysters followed them,
  And yet another four;
And thick and fast they came at last,
  And more, and more, and more—
All hopping through the frothy waves,
  And scrambling to the shore.

The Walrus and the Carpenter
  Walked on a mile or so,
And then they rested on a rock
  Conveniently low:
And all the little Oysters stood
  And waited in a row.

"The time has come," the Walrus said,
  "To talk of many things:
Of shoes—and ships—and sealing wax—
  Of cabbages—and kings—
And why the sea is boiling hot—
  And whether pigs have wings."

"But wait a bit," the Oysters cried,
  "Before we have our chat;
For some of us are out of breath,
  And all of us are fat!"

TAKE NOTES

TAKE NOTES

"No hurry!" said the Carpenter.
They thanked him much for that.

"A loaf of bread," the Walrus said,
"Is what we chiefly need:
Pepper and vinegar besides
Are very good indeed—
Now, if you're ready, Oysters dear,
We can begin to feed."

"But not on us!" the Oysters cried,
Turning a little blue.
"After such kindness, that would be
A dismal thing to do!"
"The night is fine," the Walrus said.
"Do you admire the view?"

"It was so kind of you to come!
And you are very nice!"
The Carpenter said nothing but
"Cut us another slice.
I wish you were not quite so deaf—
I've had to ask you twice!"

"It seems a shame," the Walrus said,
"To play them such a trick.
After we've brought them out so far,
And made them trot so quick!"
The Carpenter said nothing but
"The butter's spread too thick!"

"I weep for you," the Walrus said:
"I deeply sympathize."
With sobs and tears he sorted out
Those of the largest size,
Holding his pocket-handkerchief
Before his streaming eyes.

"O Oysters," said the Carpenter,
"You've had a pleasant run!
Shall we be trotting home again?"
But answer came there none—
And this was scarcely odd, because
They'd eaten every one.

Abuelito Who

by Sandra Cisneros

TAKE NOTES

Abuelito[1] who throws coins like rain
and asks who loves him
who is dough and feathers
who is a watch and glass of water
whose hair is made of fur
is too sad to come downstairs today
who tells me in Spanish you are my diamond
who tells me in English you are my sky
whose little eyes are string
can't come out to play
sleeps in his little room all night and day
who used to laugh like the letter k
is sick
is a doorknob tied to a sour stick
is tired shut the door
doesn't live here anymore
is hiding underneath the bed
who talks to me inside my head
is blankets and spoons and big brown shoes
who snores up and down up and down up and
    down again
is the rain on the roof that falls like coins
asking who loves him
who loves him who?

---

1. **Abuelito** (ä bwā lē´ tō) *n.* in Spanish, an affectionate term for a grandfather.

TAKE NOTES

April Rain Song

by Langston Hughes

Let the rain kiss you.
Let the rain beat upon your head with silver liquid drops.
Let the rain sing you a lullaby.

The rain makes still pools on the sidewalk.
The rain makes running pools in the gutter.
The rain plays a little sleep-song on our roof at night—

And I love the rain.

The World Is Not a Pleasant Place to Be

by Nikki Giovanni

TAKE NOTES

the world is not a pleasant place
to be without
someone to hold and be held by

a river would stop
its flow if only
a stream were there
to receive it

an ocean would never laugh
if clouds weren't there
to kiss her tears

the world is not
a pleasant place to be without
someone

TAKE NOTES

Fame Is a Bee

by Emily Dickinson

Fame is a bee.
It has a song—
It has a sting—
Ah, too, it has a wing.

Haiku

by Matsuo Bashõ

An old silent pond . . .
A frog jumps into the pond,
splash! Silence again.

TAKE NOTES

TAKE NOTES

The Sidewalk Racer

by Lillian Morrison

Skimming
an asphalt sea
I swerve, I curve, I
sway; I speed to whirring
sound an inch above the
ground; I'm the sailor
and the sail, I'm the
driver and the wheel
I'm the one and only
single engine
human auto
mobile.

Concrete Cat

by Dorthi Charles

A A
e r e r
stripestripestripestripe t
eYe eYe
whisker whisker stripestripestripe a i
stripestripestripestripe i l t a i l
m h whisker
whisker o t stripestripestripe
U
stripestripestripestripe

paw paw paw paw mouse

dishdish litterbox
litterbox

TAKE NOTES

TAKE NOTES

Limerick

by Anonymous

There was a young fellow named Hall,
Who fell in the spring in the fall;
'Twould have been a sad thing
If he'd died in the spring,
But he didn't—he died in the fall.

Wind and water and stone

by Octavio Paz

The water hollowed the stone,
the wind dispersed the water,
the stone stopped the wind.
Water and wind and stone.

The wind sculpted the stone,
the stone is a cup of water,
the water runs off and is wind.
Stone and wind and water.

The wind sings in its turnings,
the water murmurs as it goes,
the motionless stone is quiet.
Wind and water and stone.

One is the other, and is neither:
among their empty names
they pass and disappear,
water and stone and wind.

TAKE NOTES

TAKE NOTES

The Fairies' Lullaby

by William Shakespeare

Fairies. You spotted snakes with double tongue,
Thorny hedgehogs, be not seen.
Newts and blindworms,[1] do no wrong,
Come not near our fairy Queen.

Chorus. Philomel,[2] with melody
Sing in our sweet lullaby;
Lulla, lulla, lullaby, lulla, lulla, lullaby.
Never harm,
Nor spell, nor charm,
Come our lovely lady nigh.
So, good night, with lullaby.

Fairies. Weaving spiders, come not here.
Hence, you long-legged spinners, hence!
Beetles black, approach not near.
Worm nor snail do no offense.

Chorus. Philomel, with melody
Sing in our sweet lullaby;
Lulla, lulla, lullaby, lulla, lulla, lullaby.
Never harm,
Nor spell, nor charm,
Come our lovely lady nigh.
So, good night, with lullaby.

1. **newts** (no͞ots) **and blindworms** *n.* newts are salamanders, which look like lizards but are related to frogs. Blindworms are legless lizards.
2. **Philomel** (fil′ ə mel′) *n.* nightingale.

Cynthia in the Snow

by Gwendolyn Brooks

TAKE NOTES

It SUSHES.
It hushes
The loudness in the road.
It flitter-twitters,
And laughs away from me.
It laughs a lovely whiteness,
And whitely whirs away,
To be
Some otherwhere,
Still white as milk or shirts.
So beautiful it hurts.

TAKE NOTES

Simile: Willow and Ginkgo

by Eve Merriam

The willow is like an etching,[1]
Fine-lined against the sky.
The ginkgo is like a crude sketch,
Hardly worthy to be signed.

The willow's music is like a soprano,
Delicate and thin.
The ginkgo's tune is like a chorus
With everyone joining in.

The willow is sleek as a velvet-nosed calf;
The ginkgo is leathery as an old bull.
The willow's branches are like silken thread;
The ginkgo's like stubby rough wool.

The willow is like a nymph[2] with streaming hair;
Wherever it grows, there is green and gold and fair.
The willow dips to the water,
Protected and precious, like the king's favorite
daughter.

The ginkgo forces its way through gray concrete;
Like a city child, it grows up in the street.
Thrust against the metal sky,
Somehow it survives and even thrives.

My eyes feast upon the willow,
But my heart goes to the ginkgo.

---

1. **etching** (ech´ iŋ) *n.* print of a drawing made on metal, glass, or wood.
2. **nymph** (nimf) *n.* goddess of nature, thought of as a beautiful maiden.

Gluskabe and Old Man Winter

by Joseph Bruchac

TAKE NOTES

CHARACTERS

Speaking Roles:	Non-speaking Roles:
NARRATOR	SUN
GLUSKABE	FLOWERS
GRANDMOTHER WOODCHUCK	PLANTS
HUMAN BEING	
OLD MAN WINTER	
FOUR OR MORE SUMMER LAND PEOPLE, including the leader	
FOUR CROWS	

Scene I: *Gluskabe and Grandmother Woodchuck's Wigwam*

GLUSKABE *and* **GRANDMOTHER WOODCHUCK** *sit inside with their blankets over their shoulders.*

NARRATOR: Long ago Gluskabe (gloo-SKAH-bey) lived with his grandmother, Woodchuck, who was old and very wise. Gluskabe's job was to help the people.

GLUSKABE: It is very cold this winter, Grandmother.

GRANDMOTHER WOODCHUCK: *Ni ya yo* (nee yah yo), Grandson. You are right!

GLUSKABE: The snow is very deep, Grandmother.

GRANDMOTHER WOODCHUCK: *Ni ya yo*, Grandson.

GLUSKABE: It has been winter for a very long time, Grandmother.

GRANDMOTHER WOODCHUCK: *Ni ya yo*, Grandson. But look, here comes one of those human beings who are our friends.

TAKE NOTES

Human Being: *Kwai, Kwai, nidobak* (kwy kwy nee-DOH-bahk). Hello, my friends.

Gluskabe and **Grandmother Woodchuck:** *Kwai, Kwai, nidoba* (kwy kwy nee-DOH-bah).

Human Being: Gluskabe, I have been sent by the other human beings to ask you for help. This winter has been too long. If it does not end soon, we will all die.

Gluskabe: I will do what I can. I will go to the wigwam of Old Man Winter. He has stayed here too long. I will ask him to go back to his home in the Winter Land to the north.

Grandmother Woodchuck: Be careful, Gluskabe.

Gluskabe: Don't worry, Grandmother. Winter cannot beat me.

Scene II: *The Wigwam of Old Man Winter*

Old Man Winter *sits in his wigwam, "warming" his hands over his fire made of ice. The four balls of summer are on one side of the stage.* ***Gluskabe*** *enters stage carrying his bag and stands to the side of the wigwam door. He taps on the wigwam.*

Old Man Winter: Who is there!

Gluskabe: It is Gluskabe.

Old Man Winter: Ah, come inside and sit by my fire.

Gluskabe *enters the wigwam.*

Gluskabe: The people are suffering. You must go back to your home in the Winter Land.

Old Man Winter: Oh, I must, eh? But tell me, do you like my fire?

Gluskabe: I do not like your fire. Your fire is not warm. It is cold.

Old Man Winter: Yes, my fire is made of ice. And so are you!

Old Man Winter *throws his white sheet over* ***Gluskabe. Gluskabe*** *falls down.* ***Old Man Winter*** *stands up.*

Old Man Winter: No one can defeat me!

OLD MAN WINTER pulls GLUSKABE out of the lodge. Then he goes back inside and closes the door flap. The Sun comes out and shines on GLUSKABE. GLUSKABE sits up and looks at the Sun.

GLUSKABE: Ah, that was a good nap! But I am not going into Old Man Winter's lodge again until I talk with my grandmother.

GLUSKABE begins walking across the stage toward the four balls. GRANDMOTHER WOODCHUCK enters.

GRANDMOTHER WOODCHUCK: It is still winter, Gluskabe! Did Old Man Winter refuse to speak to you?

GLUSKABE: We spoke, but he did not listen. I will speak to him again; and I will make him listen. But tell me, Grandmother, where does the warm weather come from?

GRANDMOTHER WOODCHUCK: It is kept in the Summer Land.

GLUSKABE: I will go there and bring summer back here.

GRANDMOTHER WOODCHUCK: Grandson, the Summer Land people are strange people. Each of them has one eye. They are also greedy. They do not want to share the warm weather. It will be dangerous.

GLUSKABE: Why will it be dangerous?

GRANDMOTHER WOODCHUCK: The Summer Land people keep the summer in a big pot. They dance around it. Four giant crows guard the pot full of summer. Whenever a stranger tries to steal summer, those crows fly down and pull off his head!

GLUSKABE: Grandmother, I will go to the summer land. I will cover up one eye and look like the people there. And I will take these four balls of sinew with me.

GLUSKABE picks up the four balls, places them in his bag, and puts the bag over his shoulder.

Scene III: *The Summer Land Village*

The SUMMER LAND PEOPLE are dancing around the pot full of summer. They are singing a snake dance song, following their leader, who shakes a rattle in one hand. FOUR CROWS stand guard around the pot as the people dance.

TAKE NOTES

TAKE NOTES

Summer Land People: *Wee gai wah neh* (wee guy wah ney),

Wee gai wah neh,

Wee gai wah neh, wee gai wah neh,

Wee gai wah neh, wee gai wah neh,

Wee gai wah neh.

***Gluskabe** enters, wearing an eye patch and carrying his bag with the balls in it.*

Gluskabe: *Kwai, kwai, nidobak!* Hello, my friends.

*Everyone stops dancing. They gather around **Gluskabe**.*

Leader of The Summer Land People: Who are you?

Gluskabe: I am not a stranger. I am one of you. See, I have one eye.

Second Summer Land Person: I do not remember you.

Gluskabe: I have been gone a long time.

Third Summer Land Person: He does have only one eye.

Fourth Summer Land Person: Let's welcome him back. Come join in our snake dance.

*The singing and dancing begin again: "Wee gai wah neh," etc. **Gluskabe** is at the end of the line as the dancers circle the pot full of summer. When **Gluskabe** is close enough, he reaches in, grabs one of the summersticks, and breaks away, running back and forth.*

Leader of The Summer Land People: He has taken one of our summersticks!

Second Summer Land Person: Someone stop him!

Third Summer Land Person: Crows, catch him!

Fourth Summer Land Person: Pull off his head!

*The **Crows** swoop after **Gluskabe**. He reaches into his pouch and pulls out one of the balls. As each **Crow** comes up to him, he ducks his head down and holds up the ball. The **Crow** grabs the ball. **Gluskabe** keeps running, and pulls out another ball, repeating his actions until each of the **Crows** has grabbed a ball.*

First Crow: *Gah-gah!* I have his head.

Second Crow: *Gah-gah!* No, I have his head!

Third Crow: *Gah-gah!* Look, I have his head!

Fourth Crow: *Gah-gah!* No, look—I have it too!

Leader of The Summer Land People: How many heads did that stranger have?

Second Summer Land Person: He has tricked us. He got away.

Scene IV: *The Wigwam of Old Man Winter*

***Gluskabe** walks up to **Old Man Winter's** wigwam. He holds the summerstick in his hand and taps on the door.*

Old Man Winter: Who is there!

Gluskabe: It is Gluskabe.

Old Man Winter: Ah, come inside and sit by my fire.

Gluskabe** enters, sits, down, and places the summerstick in front of **Old Man Winter.

Gluskabe: You must go back to your home in the Winter Land.

Old Man Winter: Oh, I must, eh? But tell me, do you like my fire?

Gluskabe: Your fire is no longer cold. It is getting warmer. Your wigwam is melting away. You are getting weaker.

Old Man Winter: No one can defeat me!

Gluskabe: Old Man, you are defeated. Warm weather has returned. Go back to your home in the north.

*The blanket walls of **Old Man Winter's** wigwam collapse. **Old Man Winter** stands up and walks away as swiftly as he can, crouching down as if getting smaller. People carrying the cutouts of the Sun, Flowers, and Plants come out and surround **Gluskabe** as he sits there, smiling.*

Narrator: So Gluskabe defeated Old Man Winter. Because he brought only one small piece of summer, winter still returns each year. But, thanks to Gluskabe, spring always comes back again.

TAKE NOTES

TAKE NOTES

The Phantom Tollbooth

by Susan Nanus
based on the book by Norton Juster

Cast (in order of appearance)

- THE CLOCK
- MILO, A BOY
- THE WHETHER MAN
- SIX LETHARGARIANS
- TOCK, THE WATCHDOG (same as the clock)
- AZAZ THE UNABRIDGED, KING OF DICTIONOPOLIS
- THE MATHEMAGICIAN, KING OF DIGITOPOLIS
- PRINCESS SWEET RHYME
- PRINCESS PURE REASON
- GATEKEEPER OF DICTIONOPOLIS
- THREE WORD MERCHANTS
- THE LETTERMAN (fourth word Merchant)
- SPELLING BEE
- THE HUMBUG
- THE DUKE OF DEFINITION
- THE MINISTER OF MEANING
- THE EARL OF ESSENCE
- THE COUNT OF CONNOTATION
- THE UNDERSECRETARY OF UNDERSTANDING
- A PAGE
- KAKAFONOUS A. DISCHORD, DOCTOR OF DISSONANCE
- THE AWFUL DYNNE
- THE DODECAHEDRON
- MINERS OF THE NUMBERS MINE
- THE EVERPRESENT WORDSNATCHER
- THE TERRIBLE TRIVIUM
- THE DEMON OF INSINCERITY
- SENSES TAKER

The Sets

1. MILO'S BEDROOM—with shelves, pennants, pictures on the wall, as well as suggestions of the characters of the Land of Wisdom.
2. THE ROAD TO THE LAND OF WISDOM—a forest, from which the Whether Man and the Lethargarians emerge.
3. DICTIONOPOLIS—a marketplace full of open air stalls as well as little shops. Letters and signs should abound.
4. DIGITOPOLIS—a dark, glittering place without trees or greenery, but full of shining rocks and cliffs, with hundreds of numbers shining everywhere.

5. The Land of Ignorance—a gray, gloomy place full of cliffs and caves, with frightening faces. Different levels and heights should be suggested through one or two platforms or risers, with a set of stairs that lead to the castle in the air.

TAKE NOTES

Act I • Scene i

[*The stage is completely dark and silent. Suddenly the sound of someone winding an alarm clock is heard, and after that, the sound of loud ticking is heard.*]

[*LIGHTS UP on the* Clock, *a huge alarm clock. The* Clock *reads 4:00. The lighting should make it appear that the* Clock *is suspended in mid-air (if possible). The* Clock *ticks for 30 seconds.*]

Clock. See that! Half a minute gone by. Seems like a long time when you're waiting for something to happen, doesn't it? Funny thing is, time can pass very slowly or very fast, and sometimes even both at once. The time now? Oh, a little after four, but what that means should depend on you. Too often, we do something simply because time tells us to. Time for school, time for bed, whoops, 12:00, time to be hungry. It can get a little silly, don't you think? Time is important, but it's what you do with it that makes it so. So my advice to you is to use it. Keep your eyes open and your ears perked. Otherwise it will pass before you know it, and you'll certainly have missed something!

Things have a habit of doing that, you know. Being here one minute and gone the next.

In the twinkling of an eye.

In a jiffy.

In a flash!

I know a girl who yawned and missed a whole summer vacation. And what about that caveman who took a nap one afternoon, and woke up to find himself completely alone. You see, while he was sleeping, someone had invented the wheel and everyone had moved to the suburbs. And then of course, there is Milo. [*LIGHTS UP to reveal* Milo's *Bedroom. The* Clock *appears to be on a shelf in the room of a young boy—a room filled with books, toys,*

TAKE NOTES

games, maps, papers, pencils, a bed, a desk. There is a dartboard with numbers and the face of the MATHEMAGICIAN, *a bedspread made from* KING AZAZ'S *cloak, a kite looking like the* SPELLING BEE, *a punching bag with the* HUMBUG'S *face, as well as records, a television, a toy car, and a large box that is wrapped and has an envelope taped to the top. The sound of FOOTSTEPS is heard, and then enter* MILO *dejectedly. He throws down his books and coat, flops into a chair, and sighs loudly.*] Who never knows what to do with himself—not just sometimes, but always. When he's in school, he wants to be out, and when he's out he wants to be in. [*During the following speech,* MILO *examines the various toys, tools, and other possessions in the room, trying them out and rejecting them.*] Wherever he is, he wants to be somewhere else—and when he gets there, so what. Everything is too much trouble or a waste of time. Books—he's already read them. Games—boring. T.V.—dumb. So what's left? Another long, boring afternoon. Unless he bothers to notice a very large package that happened to arrive today.

MILO. [*Suddenly notices the package. He drags himself over to it, and disinterestedly reads the label.*] "For Milo, who has plenty of time." Well, that's true. [*Sighs and looks at it.*] No. [*Walks away.*] Well ... [*Comes back. Rips open envelope and reads.*]

A VOICE. "One genuine turnpike tollbooth, easily assembled at home for use by those who have never traveled in lands beyond."

MILO. Beyond what? [*Continues reading.*]

A VOICE. "This package contains the following items:" [MILO *pulls the items out of the box and sets them up as they are mentioned.*] "One (1) genuine turnpike tollbooth to be erected according to directions. Three (3) precautionary signs to be used in a precautionary fashion. Assorted coins for paying tolls. One (1) map, strictly up to date, showing how to get from here to there. One (1) book of rules and traffic regulations which may not be bent or broken. Warning! Results are not guaranteed. If not perfectly satisfied, your wasted time will be refunded."

MILO. [*Skeptically.*] Come off it, who do you think you're kidding? [*Walks around and examines tollbooth.*] What am I supposed to do with this? [*The ticking of the* CLOCK *grows loud and impatient.*] Well . . . what else do I have to do. [MILO *gets into his toy car and drives up to the first sign.*]

VOICE. "HAVE YOUR DESTINATION IN MIND."

MILO. [*Pulls out the map.*] Now, let's see. That's funny. I never heard of any of these places. Well, it doesn't matter anyway. Dictionopolis. That's a weird name. I might as well go there. [*Begins to move, following map. Drives off.*]

CLOCK. See what I mean? You never know how things are going to get started. But when you're bored, what you need more than anything is a rude awakening.

[*The ALARM goes off very loudly as the stage darkens. The sound of the alarm is transformed into the honking of a car horn, and is then joined by the blasts, bleeps, roars and growls of heavy highway traffic. When the lights come up,* MILO*'s bedroom is gone and we see a lonely road in the middle of nowhere.*]

Scene ii • The Road to Dictionopolis

[*Enter* MILO *in his car.*]

MILO. This is weird! I don't recognize any of this scenery at all. [*A SIGN is held up before* MILO, *startling him.*] Huh? [*Reads.*] WELCOME TO EXPECTATIONS. INFORMATION, PREDICTIONS AND ADVICE CHEERFULLY OFFERED. PARK HERE AND BLOW HORN. [MILO *blows horn.*]

WHETHER MAN. [*A little man wearing a long coat and carrying an umbrella pops up from behind the sign that he was holding. He speaks very fast and excitedly.*] My, my, my, my, my, welcome, welcome, welcome, welcome to the Land of Expectations, Expectations, Expectations! We don't get many travelers these

TAKE NOTES

TAKE NOTES

days; we certainly don't get many travelers. Now what can I do for you? I'm the Whether Man.

Milo. [*Referring to map.*] Uh . . . is this the right road to Dictionopolis?

Whether Man. Well now, well now, well now, I don't know of any wrong road to Dictionopolis, so if this road goes to Dictionopolis at all, it must be the right road, and if it doesn't, it must be the right road to somewhere else, because there are no wrong roads to anywhere. Do you think it will rain?

Milo. I thought you were the Weather Man.

Whether Man. Oh, no, I'm the Whether Man, not the weather man. [*Pulls out a SIGN or opens a FLAP of his coat, which reads: "WHETHER."*] After all, it's more important to know whether there will be weather than what the weather will be.

Milo. What kind of place is Expectations?

Whether Man. Good question, good question! Expectations is the place you must always go to before you get to where you are going. Of course, some people never go beyond Expectations, but my job is to hurry them along whether they like it or not. Now what else can I do for you? [*Opens his umbrella.*]

Milo. I think I can find my own way.

Whether Man. Splendid, splendid, splendid! Whether or not you find your own way, you're bound to find some way. If you happen to find my way, please return it. I lost it years ago. I imagine by now it must be quite rusty. You did say it was going to rain, didn't you? [*Escorts* Milo *to the car under the open umbrella.*] I'm glad you made your own decision. I do so hate to make up my mind about anything, whether it's good or bad, up or down, rain or shine. Expect everything, I always say, and the unexpected never happens. Goodbye, goodbye, goodbye, good . . .

[*A loud CLAP of THUNDER is heard.*] Oh dear! [*He looks up at the sky, puts out his hand to feel for rain, and RUNS AWAY.* Milo *watches puzzledly and drives on.*]

TAKE NOTES

be severely punished." That's a ridiculous law! Everybody thinks.

ALL THE LETHARGARIANS. We don't!

LETHARGARIAN 2. And most of the time, you don't, that's why you're here. You weren't thinking and you weren't paying attention either. People who don't pay attention often get stuck in the Doldrums. Face it, most of the time, you're just like us. [*Falls, snoring, to the ground.* MILO *laughs.*]

LETHARGARIAN 5. Stop that at once. Laughing is against the law. Don't you have a rule book? It's local ordinance 574381-W.

MILO. [*Opens rule book and reads.*] "In the Doldrums, laughter is frowned upon and smiling is permitted only on alternate Thursdays." Well, if you can't laugh or think, what can you do?

LETHARGARIAN 6. Anything as long as it's nothing, and everything as long as it isn't anything. There's lots to do. We have a very busy schedule . . .

LETHARGARIAN 1. At 8:00 we get up and then we spend from 8 to 9 daydreaming.

LETHARGARIAN 2. From 9:00 to 9:30 we take our early mid-morning nap . . .

LETHARGARIAN 3. From 9:30 to 10:30 we dawdle and delay . . .

LETHARGARIAN 4. From 10:30 to 11:30 we take our late early morning nap . . .

LETHARGARIAN 5. From 11:30 to 12:00 we bide our time and then we eat our lunch.

LETHARGARIAN 6. From 1:00 to 2:00 we linger and loiter . . .

LETHARGARIAN 1. From 2:00 to 2:30 we take our early afternoon nap . . .

LETHARGARIAN 2. From 2:30 to 3:30 we put off for tomorrow what we could have done today . . .

LETHARGARIAN 3. From 3:30 to 4:00 we take our early late afternoon nap . . .

Milo. I'd better get out of Expectations, but fast. Talking to a guy like that all day would get me nowhere for sure. [*He tries to speed up, but finds instead that he is moving slower and slower.*] Oh, oh, now what? [*He can barely move. Behind* Milo, *the* Lethargarians *begin to enter from all parts of the stage. They are dressed to blend in with the scenery and carry small pillows that look like rocks. Whenever they fall asleep, they rest on the pillows.*] Now I really am getting nowhere. I hope I didn't take a wrong turn. [*The car stops. He tries to start it. It won't move. He gets out and begins to tinker with it.*] I wonder where I am.

Lethargarian 1. You're . . . in . . . the . . . Dol . . . drums . . . [Milo *looks around.*]

Lethargarian 2. Yes . . . the . . . Dol . . . drums . . . [*A YAWN is heard.*]

Milo. [*Yelling.*] WHAT ARE THE DOLDRUMS?

Lethargarian 3. The Doldrums, my friend, are where nothing ever happens and nothing ever changes. [*Parts of the Scenery stand up or Six People come out of the scenery colored in the same colors of the trees or the road. They move very slowly and as soon as they move, they stop to rest again.*] Allow me to introduce all of us. We are the Lethargarians at your service.

Milo. [*Uncertainly.*] Very pleased to meet you. I think I'm lost. Can you help me?

Lethargarian 4. Don't say think. [*He yawns.*] It's against the law.

Lethargarian 1. No one's allowed to think in the Doldrums. [*He falls asleep.*]

Lethargarian 2. Don't you have a rule book? It's local ordinance 175389-J. [*He falls asleep.*]

Milo. [*Pulls out rule book and reads.*] Ordinance 175389-J: "It shall be unlawful, illegal and unethical to think, think of thinking, surmise, presume, reason, meditate or speculate while in the Doldrums. Anyone breaking this law shall

TAKE NOTES

Lethargarian 4. From 4:00 to 5:00 we loaf and lounge until dinner . . .

Lethargarian 5. From 6:00 to 7:00 we dilly-dally . . .

Lethargarian 6. From 7:00 to 8:00 we take our early evening nap and then for an hour before we go to bed, we waste time.

Lethargarian 1. [*Yawning.*] You see, it's really quite strenuous doing nothing all day long, and so once a week, we take a holiday and go nowhere.

Lethargarian 5. Which is just where we were going when you came along. Would you care to join us?

Milo. [*Yawning.*] That's where I seem to be going, anyway. [*Stretching.*] Tell me, does everyone here do nothing?

Lethargarian 3. Everyone but the terrible Watchdog. He's always sniffing around to see that nobody wastes time. A most unpleasant character.

Milo. The Watchdog?

Lethargarian 6. THE WATCHDOG!

All The Lethargarians. [*Yelling at once.*] RUN! WAKE UP! RUN! HERE HE COMES! THE WATCHDOG! [*They all run off and ENTER a large dog with the head, feet, and tail of a dog, and the body of a clock, having the same face as the character the* Clock.]

Watchdog. What are you doing here?

Milo. Nothing much. Just killing time. You see . . .

Watchdog. KILLING TIME! [*His ALARM RINGS in fury.*] It's bad enough wasting time without killing it. What are you doing in the Doldrums, anyway? Don't you have anywhere to go?

Milo. I think I was on my way to Dictionopolis when I got stuck here. Can you help me?

Watchdog. Help you! You've got to help yourself. I suppose you know why you got stuck.

Milo. I guess I just wasn't thinking.

Watchdog. Precisely. Now you're on your way.

TAKE NOTES

TAKE NOTES

Milo. I am?

Watchdog. Of course. Since you got here by not thinking, it seems reasonable that in order to get out, you must start thinking. Do you mind if I get in? I love automobile rides. [*He gets in. They wait.*] Well?

Milo. All right. I'll try. [*Screws up his face and thinks.*] Are we moving?

Watchdog. Not yet. Think harder.

Milo. I'm thinking as hard as I can.

Watchdog. Well, think just a little harder than that. Come on, you can do it.

Milo. All right, all right. . . . I'm thinking of all the planets in the solar system, and why water expands when it turns to ice, and all the words that begin with "q," and . . . [*The wheels begin to move.*] We're moving! We're moving!

Watchdog. Keep thinking.

Milo. [*Thinking.*] How a steam engine works and how to bake a pie and the difference between Fahrenheit and Centigrade . . .

Watchdog. Dictionopolis, here we come.

Milo. Hey, Watchdog, are you coming along?

Tock. You can call me Tock, and keep your eyes on the road.

Milo. What kind of place is Dictionopolis, anyway?

Tock. It's where all the words in the world come from. It used to be a marvelous place, but ever since Rhyme and Reason left, it hasn't been the same.

Milo. Rhyme and Reason?

Tock. The two princesses. They used to settle all the arguments between their two brothers who rule over the Land of Wisdom. You see, Azaz is the king of Dictionopolis and the Mathemagician is the king of Digitopolis and they almost never see eye to eye on anything. It was the job of the Princesses Sweet Rhyme and Pure Reason to solve the differences between the two kings, and they always did so well that both sides usually went home feeling very satisfied. But then, one day, the kings had an argument to end all arguments. . . .

[*The LIGHTS DIM on* TOCK *and* MILO, *and come up on* KING AZAZ *of Dictionopolis on another part of the stage.* AZAZ *has a great stomach, a grey beard reaching to his waist, a small crown and a long robe with the letters of the alphabet written all over it.*]

AZAZ. Of course, I'll abide by the decision of Rhyme and Reason, though I have no doubt as to what it will be. They will choose words, of course. Everyone knows that words are more important than numbers any day of the week.

[*The* MATHEMAGICIAN *appears opposite* AZAZ. *The* MATHEMAGICIAN *wears a long flowing robe covered entirely with complex mathematical equations, and a tall pointed hat. He carries a long staff with a pencil point at one end and a large rubber eraser at the other.*]

MATHEMAGICIAN. That's what you think, Azaz. People wouldn't even know what day of the week it is without numbers. Haven't you ever looked at a calendar? Face it, Azaz. It's numbers that count.

AZAZ. Don't be ridiculous. [*To audience, as if leading a cheer.*] Let's hear it for WORDS!

MATHEMAGICIAN. [To audience, in the same manner.] Cast your vote for NUMBERS!

AZAZ. A, B, C's!

MATHEMAGICIAN. 1, 2, 3's! [*A FANFARE is heard.*]

AZAZ AND **MATHEMAGICIAN.** [*To each other.*] Quiet! Rhyme and Reason are about to announce their decision.

[RHYME *and* REASON *appear.*]

RHYME. Ladies and gentlemen, letters and numerals, fractions and punctuation marks—may we have your attention, please. After careful consideration of the problem set before us by King Azaz of Dictionopolis [AZAZ *bows.*] and the Mathemagician of Digitopolis [MATHEMAGICIAN *raises his hands in a victory salute.*] we have come to the following conclusion:

TAKE NOTES

TAKE NOTES

Reason. Words and numbers are of equal value, for in the cloak of knowledge, one is the warp and the other is the woof.

Rhyme. It is no more important to count the sands than it is to name the stars.

Rhyme And Reason. Therefore, let both kingdoms, Dictionopolis and Digitopolis, live in peace.

[*The sound of CHEERING is heard.*]

Azaz. Boo! is what I say. Boo and Bah and Hiss!

Mathemagician. What good are these girls if they can't even settle an argument in anyone's favor? I think I have come to a decision of my own.

Azaz. So have I.

Azaz and **Mathemagician.** [*To the* PRINCESSES.] You are hereby banished from this land to the Castle-in-the-Air. [*To each other.*] *And as for you, KEEP OUT OF MY WAY!* [*They stalk off in opposite directions.*]

[*During this time, the set has been changed to the Market Square of Dictionopolis. LIGHTS come UP on the deserted square.*]

Tock. And ever since then, there has been neither Rhyme nor Reason in this kingdom. Words are misused and numbers are mismanaged. The argument between the two kings has divided everyone and the real value of both words and numbers has been forgotten. What a waste!

Milo. Why doesn't somebody rescue the Princesses and set everything straight again?

Tock. That is easier said than done. The Castle-in-the-Air is very far from here, and the one path which leads to it is guarded by ferocious demons. But hold on, here we are. [*A Man appears, carrying a Gate and a small Tollbooth.*]

Gatekeeper. AHHHHREMMMM! This is Dictionopolis, a happy kingdom, advantageously located in the foothills of Confusion and caressed by gentle breezes from the Sea of Knowledge. Today, by royal proclamation, is Market Day. Have you come to buy or sell?

Milo. I beg your pardon?

Gatekeeper. Buy or sell, buy or sell. Which is it? You must have come here for a reason.

Milo. Well, I . . .

Gatekeeper. Come now, if you don't have a reason, you must at least have an explanation or certainly an excuse.

Milo. [*Meekly.*] Uh . . . no.

Gatekeeper. [*Shaking his head.*] Very serious. You can't get in without a reason. [*Thoughtfully.*] Wait a minute. Maybe I have an old one you can use. [*Pulls out an old suitcase from the tollbooth and rummages through it.*] No . . . no . . . no . . . this won't do . . . hmmm . . .

Milo. [*To* Tock.] What's he looking for? [Tock *shrugs.*]

Gatekeeper. Ah! This is fine. [*Pulls out a Medallion on a chain. Engraved in the Medallion is: "WHY NOT?"*] Why not. That's a good reason for almost anything . . . a bit used, perhaps, but still quite serviceable. There you are, sir. Now I can truly say: Welcome to Dictionopolis.

[*He opens the Gate and walks off.* Citizens *and* Merchants *appear on all levels of the stage, and* Milo *and* Tock *find themselves in the middle of a noisy marketplace. As some people buy and sell their wares, others hang a large banner which reads: WELCOME TO THE WORD MARKET.*]

Milo. Tock! Look!

Merchant 1. Hey-ya, hey-ya, hey-ya, step right up and take your pick. Juicy tempting words for sale. Get your fresh-picked "if 's," "and's" and "but's"! Just take a look at these nice ripe "where's" and "when's."

Merchant 2. Step right up, step right up, fancy, best-quality words here for sale. Enrich your vocabulary and expand your speech with such elegant items as "quagmire," "flabbergast," or "upholstery."

TAKE NOTES

TAKE NOTES

Merchant 3. Words by the bag, buy them over here. Words by the bag for the more talkative customer. A pound of "happy's" at a very reasonable price ... very useful for "Happy Birthday," "Happy New Year," "happy days," or "happy-go-lucky." Or how about a package of "good's," always handy for "good morning," "good afternoon," "good evening," and "goodbye."

Milo. I can't believe it. Did you ever see so many words?

Tock. They're fine if you have something to say. [*They come to a Do-It-Yourself Bin.*]

Milo. [*To* Merchant 4 *at the bin.*] Excuse me, but what are these?

Merchant 4. These are for people who like to make up their own words. You can pick any assortment you like or buy a special box complete with all the letters and a book of instructions. Here, taste an "A." They're very good. [*He pops one into* Milo*'s mouth.*]

Milo. [*Tastes it hesitantly.*] It's sweet! [*He eats it.*]

Merchant 4. I knew you'd like it. "A" is one of our best-sellers. All of them aren't that good, you know. The "Z," for instance—very dry and sawdusty. And the "X"? Tastes like a trunkful of stale air. But most of the others aren't bad at all. Here, try the "I."

Milo. [*Tasting.*] Cool! It tastes icy.

Merchant 4. [*To* Tock.] How about the "C" for you? It's as crunchy as a bone. Most people are just too lazy to make their own words, but take it from me, not only is it more fun, but it's also *de*-lightful, [*Holds up a "D."*] *e*-lating, [*Holds up an "E."*] and extremely useful! [*Holds up a "U."*]

Milo. But isn't it difficult? I'm not very good at making words.

[*The* Spelling Bee, *a large colorful bee, comes up from behind.*]

Spelling Bee. Perhaps I can be of some assistance ... a-s-s-i-s-t-a-n-c-e. [*The Three turn around and see him.*] Don't be alarmed ... a-l-a-r-m-e-d. I am the Spelling Bee. I can spell anything. Anything. A-n-y-t-h-i-n-g. Try me. Try me.

Milo. [*Backing off,* Tock *on his guard.*] Can you spell goodbye?

Spelling Bee. Perhaps you are under the misapprehension . . . m-i-s-a-p-p-r-e-h-e-n-s-i-o-n that I am dangerous. Let me assure you that I am quite peaceful. Now, think of the most difficult word you can, and I'll spell it.

Milo. Uh . . . O.K. [*At this point,* Milo *may turn to the audience and ask them to help him choose a word or he may think of one on his own.*] How about . . . "Curiosity"?

Spelling Bee. [*Winking.*] Let's see now . . . uh . . . how much time do I have?

Milo. Just ten seconds. Count them off, Tock.

Spelling Bee. [*As* Tock *counts.*] Oh dear, oh dear. [*Just at the last moment, quickly.*] C-u-r-i-o-s-i-t-y.

Merchant 4. Correct! [All *CHEER.*]

Milo. Can you spell anything?

Spelling Bee. [*Proudly.*] Just about. You see, years ago, I was an ordinary bee minding my own business, smelling flowers all day, occasionally picking up part-time work in people's bonnets. Then one day, I realized that I'd never amount to anything without an education, so I decided that . . .

Humbug. [*Coming up in a booming voice.*] BALDERDASH! [*He wears a lavish coat, striped pants, checked vest, spats and a derby hat.*] Let me repeat . . . BALDERDASH! [*Swings his cane and clicks his heels in the air.*] Well, well, what have we here? Isn't someone going to introduce me to the little boy?

Spelling Bee. [*Disdainfully.*] This is the Humbug. You can't trust a word he says.

Humbug. NONSENSE! Everyone can trust a Humbug. As I was saying to the king just the other day . . .

Spelling Bee. You've never met the king. [*To* Milo.] Don't believe a thing he tells you.

Humbug. Bosh, my boy, pure bosh. The Humbugs are an old and noble family, honorable to the core.

TAKE NOTES

TAKE NOTES

Why, we fought in the Crusades with Richard the Lionhearted, crossed the Atlantic with Columbus, blazed trails with the pioneers. History is full of Humbugs.

Spelling Bee. A very pretty speech . . . s-p-e-e-c-h. Now, why don't you go away? I was just advising the lad of the importance of proper spelling.

Humbug. BAH! As soon as you learn to spell one word, they ask you to spell another. You can never catch up, so why bother? [*Puts his arm around* Milo.] Take my advice, boy, and forget about it. As my great-great-great-grandfather George Washington Humbug used to say . . .

Spelling Bee. You, sir, are an impostor i-m-p-o-s-t-o-r who can't even spell his own name!

Humbug. What? You dare to doubt my word? The word of a Humbug? The word of a Humbug who has direct access to the ear of a King? And the king shall hear of this, I promise you . . .

Voice 1. Did someone call for the King?

Voice 2. Did you mention the monarch?

Voice 3. Speak of the sovereign?

Voice 4. Entreat the Emperor?

Voice 5. Hail his highness?

[*Five tall, thin gentlemen regally dressed in silks and satins, plumed hats and buckled shoes appear as they speak.*]

Milo. Who are they?

Spelling Bee. The King's advisors. Or in more formal terms, his cabinet.

Minister 1. Greetings!

Minister 2. Salutations!

Minister 3. Welcome!

Minister 4. Good Afternoon!

Minister 5. Hello!

Milo. Uh . . . Hi.

[*All the* MINISTERS, *from here on called by their numbers, unfold their scrolls and read in order.*]

MINISTER 1. By the order of Azaz the Unabridged . . .

MINISTER 2. King of Dictionopolis . . .

MINISTER 3. Monarch of letters . . .

MINISTER 4. Emperor of phrases, sentences, and miscellaneous figures of speech . . .

MINISTER 5. We offer you the hospitality of our kingdom . . .

MINISTER 1. Country

MINISTER 2. Nation

MINISTER 3. State

MINISTER 4. Commonwealth

MINISTER 5. Realm

MINISTER 1. Empire

MINISTER 2. Palatinate

MINISTER 3. Principality.

MILO. Do all those words mean the same thing?

MINISTER 1. Of course.

MINISTER 2. Certainly.

MINISTER 3. Precisely.

MINISTER 4. Exactly.

MINISTER 5. Yes.

MILO. Then why don't you use just one? Wouldn't that make a lot more sense?

MINISTER 1. Nonsense!

MINISTER 2. Ridiculous!

MINISTER 3. Fantastic!

MINISTER 4. Absurd!

MINISTER 5. Bosh!

MINISTER 1. We're not interested in making sense. It's not our job.

TAKE NOTES

TAKE NOTES

Minister 2. Besides, one word is as good as another, so why not use them all?

Minister 3. Then you don't have to choose which one is right.

Minister 4. Besides, if one is right, then ten are ten times as right.

Minister 5. Obviously, you don't know who we are.

[*Each presents himself and* Milo *acknowledges the introduction.*]

Minister 1. The Duke of Definition.

Minister 2. The Minister of Meaning.

Minister 3. The Earl of Essence.

Minister 4. The Count of Connotation.

Minister 5. The Undersecretary of Understanding.

All Five. And we have come to invite you to the Royal Banquet.

Spelling Bee. The banquet! That's quite an honor, my boy. A real h-o-n-o-r.

Humbug. DON'T BE RIDICULOUS! Everybody goes to the Royal Banquet these days.

Spelling Bee. [*To the* Humbug.] True, everybody does go. But some people are invited and others simply push their way in where they aren't wanted.

Humbug. HOW DARE YOU? You buzzing little upstart, I'll show you who's not wanted . . . [*Raises his cane threateningly.*]

Spelling Bee. You just watch it! I'm warning w-a-r-n-i-n-g you! [*At that moment, an ear-shattering blast of TRUMPETS, entirely off-key, is heard, and a* Page *appears.*]

Page. King Azaz the Unabridged is about to begin the Royal banquet. All guests who do not appear promptly at the table will automatically lose their place. [*A huge Table is carried out with* King Azaz *sitting in a large chair, carried out at the head of the table.*]

TAKE NOTES

Azaz. Places. Everyone take your places. [*All the characters, including the* Humbug *and the* Spelling Bee, *who forget their quarrel, rush to take their places at the table.* Milo *and* Tock *sit near the king.* Azaz *looks at* Milo.] And just who is this?

Milo. Your Highness, my name is Milo and this is Tock. Thank you very much for inviting us to your banquet, and I think your palace is beautiful!

Minister 1. Exquisite.

Minister 2. Lovely.

Minister 3. Handsome.

Minister 4. Pretty.

Minister 5. Charming.

Azaz. SILENCE! Now tell me, young man, what can you do to entertain us? Sing songs? Tell stories? Juggle plates? Do tumbling tricks? Which is it?

Milo. I can't do any of those things.

Azaz. What an ordinary little boy. Can't you do anything at all?

Milo. Well . . . I can count to a thousand.

Azaz. AARGH, numbers! Never mention numbers here. Only use them when we absolutely have to. Now, why don't we change the subject and have some dinner? Since you are the guest of honor, you may pick the menu.

Milo. Me? Well, uh . . . I'm not very hungry. Can we just have a light snack?

Azaz. A light snack it shall be!

[Azaz *claps his hands. Waiters rush in with covered trays. When they are uncovered, Shafts of Light pour out. The light may be created through the use of battery-operated flashlights which are secured in the trays and covered with a false bottom. The Guests help themselves.*]

Humbug. Not a very substantial meal. Maybe you can suggest something a little more filling.

TAKE NOTES

Milo. Well, in that case, I think we ought to have a square meal. . . .

Azaz. [*Claps his hands.*] A square meal it is! [*Waiters serve trays of Colored Squares of all sizes. People serve themselves.*]

Spelling Bee. These are awful. [Humbug *coughs and all the Guests do not care for the food.*]

Azaz. [*Claps his hands and the trays are removed.*] Time for speeches. [*To* Milo.] You first.

Milo. [*Hesitantly.*] Your Majesty, ladies and gentlemen, I would like to take this opportunity to say that . . .

Azaz. That's quite enough. Mustn't talk all day.

Milo. But I just started to . . .

Azaz. NEXT!

Humbug. [*Quickly.*] Roast turkey, mashed potatoes, vanilla ice cream.

Spelling Bee. Hamburgers, corn on the cob, chocolate pudding p-u-d-d-i-n-g. [*Each Guest names two dishes and a dessert.*]

Azaz. [*The last.*] Pâté de foie gras, soupe à l'oignon, salade endives, fromage et fruits et demi-tasse. [*He claps his hands. Waiters serve each Guest his Words.*] Dig in. [*To* Milo.] Though I can't say I think much of your choice.

Milo. I didn't know I was going to have to eat my words.

Azaz. Of course, of course, everybody here does. Your speech should have been in better taste.

Minister 1. Here, try some somersault. It improves the flavor.

Minister 2. Have a rigamarole. [*Offers breadbasket.*]

Minister 3. Or a ragamuffin.

Minister 4. Perhaps you'd care for a synonym bun.

Minister 5. Why not wait for your just desserts?

Azaz. Ah yes, the dessert. We're having a special treat today . . . freshly made at the half-bakery.

Milo. The half-bakery?

Azaz. Of course, the half-bakery! Where do you think half-baked ideas come from? Now, please don't interrupt. By royal command, the pastry chefs have . . .

Milo. What's a half-baked idea?

[Azaz *gives up the idea of speaking as a cart is wheeled in and the Guests help themselves.*]

Humbug. They're very tasty, but they don't always agree with you. Here's a good one. [Humbug *hands one to* Milo.]

Milo. [*Reads.*] "The earth is flat."

Spelling Bee. People swallowed that one for years. [*Picks up one and reads.*] "The moon is made of green cheese." Now, there's a half-baked idea.

[*Everyone chooses one and eats. They include: "It Never Rains But Pours," "Night Air Is Bad Air," "Everything Happens for the Best," "Coffee Stunts Your Growth."*]

Azaz. And now for a few closing words. Attention! Let me have your attention! [*Everyone leaps up and Exits, except for* Milo, Tock, *and the* Humbug.] Loyal subjects and friends, once again on this gala occasion, we have . . .

Milo. Excuse me, but everybody left.

Azaz. [*Sadly.*] I was hoping no one would notice. It happens every time.

Humbug. They're gone to dinner, and as soon as I finish this last bite, I shall join them.

Milo. That's ridiculous. How can they eat dinner right after a banquet?

Azaz. SCANDALOUS! We'll put a stop to it at once. From now on, by royal command, everyone must eat dinner before the banquet.

Milo. But that's just as bad.

Humbug. Or just as good. Things which are equally bad are also equally good. Try to look at the bright side of things.

TAKE NOTES

TAKE NOTES

Milo. I don't know which side of anything to look at. Everything is so confusing, and all your words only make things worse.

Azaz. How true. There must be something we can do about it.

Humbug. Pass a law.

Azaz. We have almost as many laws as words.

Humbug. Offer a reward. [Azaz *shakes his head and looks madder at each suggestion.*] Send for help? Drive a bargain? Pull the switch? Lower the boom? Toe the line?

[*As* Azaz *continues to scowl, the* Humbug *loses confidence and finally gives up.*]

Milo. Maybe you should let Rhyme and Reason return.

Azaz. How nice that would be. Even if they were a bother at times, things always went so well when they were here. But I'm afraid it can't be done.

Humbug. Certainly not. Can't be done.

Milo. Why not?

Humbug. [*Now siding with* Milo.] Why not, indeed?

Azaz. Much too difficult.

Humbug. Of course, much too difficult.

Milo. You could, if you really wanted to.

Humbug. By all means, if you really wanted to, you could.

Azaz. [*To* Humbug.] How?

Milo. [*Also to* Humbug.] Yeah, how?

Humbug. Why ... uh, it's a simple task for a brave boy with a stout heart, a steadfast dog and a serviceable small automobile.

Azaz. Go on.

Humbug. Well, all that he would have to do is cross the dangerous, unknown countryside between here and Digitopolis, where he would have to persuade the Mathemagician to release the Princesses, which we know to be impossible because the Mathemagician will never agree with Azaz about anything. Once achieving that, it's a simple matter of entering the Mountains of Ignorance from where no one has ever returned alive, an effortless climb up a two thousand foot stairway without railings in a high wind at night to the Castle-in-the-Air. After a pleasant chat with the Princesses, all that remains is a leisurely ride back through those chaotic crags where the frightening fiends have sworn to tear any intruder limb from limb and devour him down to his belt buckle. And finally after doing all that, a triumphal parade! If, of course, there is anything left to parade . . . followed by hot chocolate and cookies for everyone.

Azaz. I never realized it would be so simple.

Milo. It sounds dangerous to me.

Tock. And just who is supposed to make that journey?

Azaz. A very good question. But there is one far more serious problem.

Milo. What's that?

Azaz. I'm afraid I can't tell you that until you return.

Milo. But wait a minute, I didn't . . .

Azaz. Dictionopolis will always be grateful to you, my boy, and your dog. [Azaz *pats* Tock *and* Milo.]

Tock. Now, just one moment, sire . . .

Azaz. You will face many dangers on your journey, but fear not, for I can give you something for your protection. [Azaz *gives* Milo *a box.*] In this box are the letters of the alphabet. With them you can form all the words you will ever need to help you overcome the obstacles that may stand in your path. All you must do is use them well and in the right places.

Milo. [*Miserably.*] Thanks a lot.

Azaz. You will need a guide, of course, and since he knows the obstacles so well, the Humbug has cheerfully volunteered to accompany you.

Humbug. Now, see here . . . !

TAKE NOTES

TAKE NOTES

Azaz. You will find him dependable, brave, resourceful and loyal.

Humbug. [*Flattered.*] Oh, your Majesty.

Milo. I'm sure he'll be a great help. [*They approach the car.*]

Tock. I hope so. It looks like we're going to need it.

[*The lights darken and the* KING *fades from view.*]

Azaz. Good luck! Drive carefully! [*The three get into the car and begin to move. Suddenly a thunderously loud NOISE is heard. They slow down the car.*]

Milo. What was that?

Tock. It came from up ahead.

Humbug. It's something terrible, I just know it. Oh, no. Something dreadful is going to happen to us. I can feel it in my bones. [*The NOISE is repeated. They all look at each other fearfully as the lights fade.*]

The Phantom Tollbooth

by Susan Nanus
based on the book by Norton Juster

TAKE NOTES

Review and Anticipate

In Act I, Milo is lifted from his boredom into a strange kingdom that is in conflict over the importance of letters and numbers. After traveling through Dictionopolis, he agrees to rescue the princesses who can settle the conflict. As Act II opens, Milo enters Digitopolis with Tock and Humbug—characters who will help him rescue the princesses.

Act II • Scene i

[*The set of Digitopolis glitters in the background, while Upstage Right near the road, a small colorful Wagon sits, looking quite deserted. On its side in large letters, a sign reads: "KAKAFONOUS A. DISCHORD Doctor of* Dissonance." *Enter* MILO, TOCK, *and* HUMBUG, *fearfully. They look at the wagon.*]

TOCK. There's no doubt about it. That's where the noise was coming from.

HUMBUG. [*To* MILO.] Well, go on.

MILO. Go on what?

HUMBUG. Go on and see who's making all that noise in there. We can't just ignore a creature like that.

MILO. Creature? What kind of creature? Do you think he's dangerous?

HUMBUG. Go on, Milo. Knock on the door. We'll be right behind you.

MILO. O.K. Maybe he can tell us how much further it is to Digitopolis.

[MILO *tiptoes up to the wagon door and KNOCKS timidly. The moment he knocks, a terrible CRASH is heard inside the wagon, and* MILO *and the others jump back in fright. At the same time, the Door Flies Open, and from the dark interior, a Hoarse* VOICE *inquires.*]

TAKE NOTES

Voice. Have you ever heard a whole set of dishes dropped from the ceiling onto a hard stone floor? [*The Others are speechless with fright.* Milo *shakes his head.* Voice *happily.*] Have you ever heard an ant wearing fur slippers walk across a thick wool carpet? [Milo *shakes his head again.*] Have you ever heard a blindfolded octopus unwrap a cellophane-covered bathtub? [Milo *shakes his head a third time.*] Ha! I knew it. [*He hops out, a little man, wearing a white coat, with a stethoscope around his neck, and a small mirror attached to his forehead, and with very huge ears, and a mortar and pestle in his hands. He stares at* Milo, Tock *and* Humbug.] None of you looks well at all! Tsk, tsk, not at all. [*He opens the top or side of his Wagon, revealing a dusty interior resembling an old apothecary shop, with shelves lined with jars and boxes, a table, books, test tubes and bottles and measuring spoons.*]

Milo. [*Timidly.*] Are you a doctor?

Dischord. [Voice.] I am KAKAFONOUS A. DISCHORD, DOCTOR OF DISSONANCE! [*Several small explosions and a grinding crash are heard.*]

Humbug. [*Stuttering with fear.*] What does the "A" stand for?

Dischord. AS LOUD AS POSSIBLE! [*Two screeches and a bump are heard.*] Now, step a little closer and stick out your tongues. [Dischord *examines them.*] Just as I expected. [*He opens a large dusty book and thumbs through the pages.*] You're all suffering from a severe lack of noise. [Dischord *begins running around, collecting bottles, reading the labels to himself as he goes along.*] "Loud Cries." "Soft Cries." "Bangs, Bongs, Swishes. Swooshes." "Snaps and Crackles." "Whistles and Gongs." "Squeeks, Squawks, and Miscellaneous Uproar." [*As he reads them off, he pours a little of each into a large glass beaker and stirs the mixture with a wooden spoon. The concoction smokes and bubbles.*] Be ready in just a moment.

Milo. [*Suspiciously.*] Just what kind of doctor are you?

Dischord. Well, you might say, I'm a specialist. I specialize in noises, from the loudest to the softest, and from the slightly annoying to the terribly unpleasant. For instance, have you ever heard a square-wheeled steamroller ride over a street full of hard-boiled eggs? [*Very loud CRUNCHING SOUNDS are heard.*]

Milo. [*Holding his ears.*] But who would want all those terrible noises?

Dischord. [*Surprised at the question.*] Everybody does. Why, I'm so busy I can hardly fill all the orders for noise pills, racket lotion, clamor salve and hubbub tonic. That's all people seem to want these days. Years ago, everyone wanted pleasant sounds and business was terrible. But then the cities were built and there was a great need for honking horns, screeching trains, clanging bells and all the rest of those wonderfully unpleasant sounds we use so much today. I've been working overtime ever since and my medicine here is in great demand. All you have to do is take one spoonful every day, and you'll never have to hear another beautiful sound again. Here, try some.

Humbug. [*Backing away.*] If it's all the same to you, I'd rather not.

Milo. I don't want to be cured of beautiful sounds.

Tock. Besides, there's no such sickness as a lack of noise.

Dischord. How true. That's what makes it so difficult to cure. [*Takes a large glass bottle from the shelf.*] Very well, if you want to go all through life suffering from a noise deficiency, I'll just give this to Dynne for his lunch. [*Uncorks the bottle and pours the liquid into it. There is a rumbling and then a loud explosion accompanied by smoke, out of which* DYNNE, *a smog-like creature with yellow eyes and a frowning mouth, appears.*]

Dynne. [*Smacking his lips.*] Ahhh, that was good, Master. I thought you'd never let me out. It was really cramped in there.

TAKE NOTES

TAKE NOTES

Dischord. This is my assistant, the awful Dynne. You must forgive his appearance, for he really doesn't have any.

Milo. What is a Dynne?

Dischord. You mean you've never heard of the awful Dynne? When you're playing in your room and making a great amount of noise, what do they tell you to stop?

Milo. That awful din.

Dischord. When the neighbors are playing their radio too loud late at night, what do you wish they'd turn down?

Tock. That awful din.

Dischord. And when the street on your block is being repaired and the drills are working all day, what does everyone complain of?

Humbug. [*Brightly.*] The dreadful row.

Dynne. The Dreadful Rauw was my grandfather. He perished in the great silence epidemic of 1712. I certainly can't understand why you don't like noise. Why, I heard an explosion last week that was so lovely, I groaned with appreciation for two days. [*He gives a loud groan at the memory.*]

Dischord. He's right, you know! Noise is the most valuable thing in the world.

Milo. King Azaz says words are.

Dischord. NONSENSE! Why, when a baby wants food, how does he ask?

Dynne. [*Happily.*] He screams!

Dischord. And when a racing car wants gas?

Dynne. [*Jumping for joy.*] It chokes!

Dischord. And what happens to the dawn when a new day begins?

Dynne. [*Delighted.*] It breaks!

Dischord. You see how simple it is? [*To* Dynne.] Isn't it time for us to go?

Milo. Where to? Maybe we're going the same way.

Dynne. I doubt it. [*Picking up empty sacks from the table.*] We're going on our collection rounds. Once a day, I travel throughout the kingdom and collect all the wonderfully horrible and beautifully unpleasant sounds I can find and bring them back to the doctor to use in his medicine.

Dischord. Where are you going?

Milo. To Digitopolis.

Dischord. Oh, there are a number of ways to get to Digitopolis, if you know how to follow directions. Just take a look at the sign at the fork in the road. Though why you'd ever want to go there, I'll never know.

Milo. We want to talk to the Mathemagician.

Humbug. About the release of the Princesses Rhyme and Reason.

Dischord. Rhyme and Reason? I remember them. Very nice girls, but a little too quiet for my taste. In fact, I've been meaning to send them something that Dynne brought home by mistake and which I have absolutely no use for. [*He rummages through the wagon.*] Ah, here it is . . . or maybe you'd like it for yourself. [*Hands* Milo *a Package.*]

Milo. What is it?

Dischord. The sounds of laughter. They're so unpleasant to hear, it's almost unbearable. All those giggles and snickers and happy shouts of joy, I don't know what Dynne was thinking of when he collected them. Here, take them to the Princesses or keep them for yourselves, I don't care. Well, time to move on. Goodbye now and good luck! [*He has shut the wagon by now and gets in. LOUD NOISES begin to erupt as* Dynne *pulls the wagon offstage.*]

Milo. [*Calling after them.*] But wait! The fork in the road . . . you didn't tell us where it is. . . .

Tock. It's too late. He can't hear a thing.

Humbug. I could use a fork of my own, at the moment. And a knife and a spoon to go with it. All of a sudden, I feel very hungry.

TAKE NOTES

TAKE NOTES

Milo. So do I, but it's no use thinking about it. There won't be anything to eat until we reach Digitopolis. [*They get into the car.*]

Humbug. [*Rubbing his stomach.*] Well, the sooner the better is what I say. [*A SIGN suddenly appears.*]

Voice. [*A strange voice from nowhere.*] But which way will get you there sooner? That is the question.

Tock. Did you hear something?

Milo. Look! The fork in the road and a signpost to Digitopolis! [*They read the Sign.*]

Humbug. Let's travel by miles, it's shorter.

Milo. Let's travel by half inches. It's quicker.

Tock. But which road should we take? It must make a difference.

Milo. Do you think so?

Tock. Well, I'm not sure, but . . .

Humbug. He could be right. On the other hand, he could also be wrong. Does it make a difference or not?

Voice. Yes, indeed, indeed it does, certainly, my yes, it does make a difference.

[*The* DODECAHEDRON *appears, a 12-sided figure with a different face on each side, and with all the edges labeled with a small letter and all the angles labeled with a large letter. He wears a beret and peers at the others with a serious face. He doffs his cap and recites:*]

Dodecahedron. *My angles are many.*
My sides are not few.
I'm the Dodecahedron.
Who are you?

Milo. What's a Dodecahedron?

Dodecahedron. [*Turning around slowly.*] See for yourself. A Dodecahedron is a mathematical shape with 12 faces. [*All his faces appear as he turns, each face with a different expression. He points to them.*] I usually use one at a time. It saves wear and tear. What are you called?

Milo. Milo.

Dodecahedron. That's an odd name. [*Changing his smiling face to a frowning one.*] And you have only one face.

Milo. [*Making sure it is still there.*] Is that bad?

Dodecahedron. You'll soon wear it out using it for everything. Is everyone with one face called Milo?

Milo. Oh, no. Some are called Billy or Jeffery or Sally or Lisa or lots of other things.

Dodecahedron. How confusing. Here everything is called exactly what it is. The triangles are called triangles, the circles are called circles, and even the same numbers have the same name. Can you imagine what would happen if we named all the twos Billy or Jeffery or Sally or Lisa or lots of other things? You'd have to say Robert plus John equals four, and if the fours were named Albert, things would be hopeless.

Milo. I never thought of it that way.

Dodecahedron. [*With an admonishing face.*] Then I suggest you begin at once, for in Digitopolis, everything is quite precise.

Milo. Then perhaps you can help us decide which road we should take.

Dodecahedron. [*Happily.*] By all means. There's nothing to it. [*As he talks, the three others try to solve the problem on a Large Blackboard that is wheeled onstage for the occasion.*] Now, if a small car carrying three people at 30 miles an hour for 10 minutes along a road 5 miles long at 11:35 in the morning starts at the same time as 3 people who have been traveling in a little automobile at 20 miles an hour for 15 minutes on another road exactly twice as long as half the distance of the other, while a dog, a bug, and a boy travel an equal distance in the same time or the same distance in an equal time along a third road in mid-October, then which one arrives first and which is the best way to go?

Humbug. Seventeen!

Milo. [*Still figuring frantically.*] I'm not sure, but . . .

Dodecahedron. You'll have to do better than that.

TAKE NOTES

TAKE NOTES

Milo. I'm not very good at problems.

Dodecahedron. What a shame. They're so very useful. Why, did you know that if a beaver 2 feet long with a tail a foot and a half long can build a dam 12 feet high and 6 feet wide in 2 days, all you would need to build Boulder Dam is a beaver 68 feet long with a 51 foot tail?

Humbug. [*Grumbling as his pencil snaps.*] Where would you find a beaver that big?

Dodecahedron. I don't know, but if you did, you'd certainly know what to do with him.

Milo. That's crazy.

Dodecahedron. That may be true, but it's completely accurate, and as long as the answer is right, who cares if the question is wrong?

Tock. [*Who has been patiently doing the first problem.*] All three roads arrive at the same place at the same time.

Dodecahedron. Correct! And I'll take you there myself. [*The blackboard rolls off, and all four get into the car and drive off.*] Now you see how important problems are. If you hadn't done this one properly, you might have gone the wrong way.

Milo. But if all the roads arrive at the same place at the same time, then aren't they all the right road?

Dodecahedron. [*Glaring from his upset face.*] Certainly not! They're all the wrong way! Just because you have a choice, it doesn't mean that any of them has to be right. [*Pointing in another direction.*] That's the way to Digitopolis and we'll be there any moment. [*Suddenly the lighting grows dimmer.*] In fact, we're here. Welcome to the Land of Numbers.

Humbug. [*Looking around at the barren landscape.*] It doesn't look very inviting.

Milo. Is this the place where numbers are made?

Dodecahedron. They're not made. You have to dig for them. Don't you know anything at all about numbers?

Milo. Well, I never really thought they were very important.

Dodecahedron. NOT IMPORTANT! Could you have tea for two without the 2? Or three blind mice without the 3? And how would you sail the seven seas without the 7?

Milo. All I meant was . . .

Dodecahedron. [*Continues shouting angrily.*] If you had high hopes, how would you know how high they were? And did you know that narrow escapes come in different widths? Would you travel the whole world wide without ever knowing how wide it was? And how could you do anything at long last without knowing how long the last was? Why, numbers are the most beautiful and valuable things in the world. Just follow me and I'll show you. [*He motions to them and pantomimes walking through rocky terrain with the others in tow. A Doorway similar to the Tollbooth appears and the* Dodecahedron *opens it and motions the others to follow him through.*] Come along, come along. I can't wait for you all day. [*They enter the doorway and the lights are dimmed very low, as to simulate the interior of a cave. The SOUNDS of scrapings and tapping, scuffling and digging are heard all around them. He hands them Helmets with flashlights attached.*] Put these on.

Milo. [*Whispering.*] Where are we going?

Dodecahedron. We're here. This is the numbers mine. [*LIGHTS UP A LITTLE, revealing Little Men digging and chopping, shoveling and scraping.*] Right this way and watch your step. [*His voice echoes and reverberates. Iridescent and glittery numbers seem to sparkle from everywhere.*]

Milo. [*Awed.*] Whose mine is it?

Voice of Mathemagician. By the four million eight hundred and twenty-seven thousand six hundred and fifty-nine hairs on my head, it's mine, of course! [*ENTER the* Mathemagician, *carrying his long staff which looks like a giant pencil.*]

Humbug. [*Already intimidated.*] It's a lovely mine, really it is.

Mathemagician. [*Proudly.*] The biggest number mine in the kingdom.

TAKE NOTES

TAKE NOTES

Milo. [*Excitedly.*] Are there any precious stones in it?

Mathemagician. Precious stones! [*Then softly.*] By the eight million two hundred and forty-seven thousand three hundred and twelve threads in my robe, I'll say there are. Look here. [*Reaches in a cart, pulls out a small object, polishes it vigorously and holds it to the light, where it sparkles.*]

Milo. But that's a five.

Mathemagician. Exactly. As valuable a jewel as you'll find anywhere. Look at some of the others. [*Scoops up others and pours them into* Milo's *arms. They include all numbers from 1 to 9 and an assortment of zeros.*]

Dodecahedron. We dig them and polish them right here, and then send them all over the world. Marvelous, aren't they?

Tock. They are beautiful. [*He holds them up to compare them to the numbers on his clock body.*]

Milo. So that's where they come from. [*Looks at them and carefully hands them back, but drops a few which smash and break in half.*] Oh, I'm sorry!

Mathemagician. [*Scooping them up.*] Oh, don't worry about that. We use the broken ones for fractions. How about some lunch? [*Takes out a little whistle and blows it. Two miners rush in carrying an immense cauldron which is bubbling and steaming. The workers put down their tools and gather around to eat.*]

Humbug. That looks delicious! [Tock *and* Milo *also look hungrily at the pot.*]

Mathemagician. Perhaps you'd care for something to eat?

Milo. Oh, yes, sir!

Tock. Thank you.

Humbug. [*Already eating.*] Ummm . . . delicious! [*All finish their bowls immediately.*]

Mathemagician. Please have another portion. [*They eat and finish.* Mathemagician *serves them again.*] Don't stop now. [*They finish.*] Come on, no need to be bashful. [*Serves them again.*]

Milo. [*To* Tock *and* Humbug *as he finishes again.*] Do you want to hear something strange? Each one I eat makes me a little hungrier than before.

Mathemagician. Do have some more. [*He serves them again. They eat frantically, until the* Mathemagician *blows his whistle again and the pot is removed.*]

Humbug. [*Holding his stomach.*] Uggghhh! I think I'm starving.

Milo. Me, too, and I ate so much.

Dodecahedron. [*Wiping the gravy from several of his mouths.*] Yes, it was delicious, wasn't it? It's the specialty of the kingdom . . . subtraction stew.

Tock. [*Weak from hunger.*] I have more of an appetite than when I began.

Mathemagician. Certainly, what did you expect? The more you eat, the hungrier you get, everyone knows that.

Milo. They do? Then how do you get enough?

Mathemagician. Enough? Here in Digitopolis, we have our meals when we're full and eat until we're hungry. That way, when you don't have anything at all, you have more than enough. It's a very economical system. You must have been stuffed to havc caten so much.

Dodecahedron. It's completely logical. The more you want, the less you get, and the less you get, the more you have. Simple arithmetic, that's all. [Tock, Milo *and* Humbug *look at him blankly.*] Now, look, suppose you had something and added nothing to it. What would you have?

Milo. The same.

Dodecahedron. Splendid! And suppose you had something and added less than nothing to it? What would you have then?

Humbug. Starvation! Oh, I'm so hungry.

TAKE NOTES

TAKE NOTES

Dodecahedron. Now, now, it's not as bad as all that. In a few hours, you'll be nice and full again ... just in time for dinner.

Milo. But I only eat when I'm hungry.

Mathemagician. [*Waving the eraser of his staff.*] What a curious idea. The next thing you'll have us believe is that you only sleep when you're tired.

[*The mine has disappeared as well as the Miners.*]

Humbug. Where did everyone go?

Mathemagician. Oh, they're still in the mine. I often find that the best way to get from one place to another is to erase everything and start again. Please make yourself at home.

[*They find themselves in a unique room, in which all the walls, tables, chairs, desks, cabinets and blackboards are labeled to show their heights, widths, depths and distances to and from each other. To one side is a gigantic notepad on an artist's easel, and from hooks and strings hang a collection of rulers, measures, weights and tapes, and all other measuring devices.*]

Milo. Do you always travel that way? [*He looks around in wonder.*]

Mathemagician. No, indeed! [*He pulls a plumb line from a hook and walks.*] Most of the time I take the shortest distance between any two points. And of course, when I have to be in several places at once ... [*He writes 3 x 1 = 3 on the notepad with his staff.*] I simply multiply. [Three figures *looking like the* Mathemagician *appear on a platform above.*]

Milo. How did you do that?

Mathemagician and The Three. There's nothing to it, if you have a magic staff. [*The* three figures *cancel themselves out and disappear.*]

Humbug. That's nothing but a big pencil.

Mathemagician. True enough, but once you learn to use it, there's no end to what you can do.

Milo. Can you make things disappear?

Mathemagician. Just step a little closer and watch this. [*Shows them that there is nothing up his sleeve or in his hat. He writes:*] 4 + 9 - 2 x 16 + 1 = 3 x 6 - 67 + 8 x 2 - 3 + 26 - 1 - 34 + 3 - 7 + 2 - 5 = [*He looks up expectantly.*]

Humbug. Seventeen?

Milo. It all comes to zero.

Mathemagician. Precisely. [*Makes a theatrical bow and rips off paper from notepad.*] Now, is there anything else you'd like to see? [*At this point, an appeal to the audience to see if anyone would like a problem solved.*]

Milo. Well . . . can you show me the biggest number there is?

Mathemagician. Why, I'd be delighted. [*Opening a closet door.*] We keep it right here. It took four miners to dig it out. [*He shows them a huge "3" twice as high as the* **Mathemagician.**]

Milo. No, that's not what I mean. Can you show me the longest number there is?

Mathemagician. Sure. [*Opens another door.*] Here it is. It took three carts to carry it here. [*Door reveals an "8" that is as wide as the "3" was high.*]

Milo. No, no, that's not what I meant either. [*Looks helplessly at* Tock.]

Tock. I think what you would like to see is the number of the greatest possible magnitude.

Mathemagician. Well, why didn't you say so? [*He busily measures them and all other things as he speaks, and marks it down.*] What's the greatest number you can think of? [*Here, an appeal can also be made to the audience or* Milo *may think of his own answers.*]

Milo. Uh . . . nine trillion, nine hundred and ninety-nine billion, nine hundred ninety-nine million, nine-hundred ninety-nine thousand, nine hundred and ninety-nine [*He puffs.*]

Mathemagician. [*Writes that on the pad.*] Very good. Now add one to it. [Milo *or audience does.*] Now add

TAKE NOTES

TAKE NOTES

one again. [Milo *or audience does so.*] Now add one again. Now add one again. Now add . . .

Milo. But when can I stop?

Mathemagician. Never. Because the number you want is always at least one more than the number you have, and it's so large that if you started saying it yesterday, you wouldn't finish tomorrow.

Humbug. Where could you ever find a number so big?

Mathemagician. In the same place they have the smallest number there is, and you know what that is?

Milo. The smallest number . . . let's see . . . one one-millionth?

Mathemagician. Almost. Now all you have to do is divide that in half and then divide that in half and then divide that in half and then divide that . . .

Milo. Doesn't that ever stop either?

Mathemagician. How can it when you can always take half of what you have and divide it in half again? Look. [*Pointing offstage.*] You see that line?

Milo. You mean that long one out there?

Mathemagician. That's it. Now, if you just follow that line forever, and when you reach the end, turn left, you will find the Land of Infinity. That's where the tallest, the shortest, the biggest, the smallest and the most and the least of everything are kept.

Milo. But how can you follow anything forever? You know, I get the feeling that everything in Digitopolis is very difficult.

Mathemagician. But on the other hand, I think you'll find that the only thing you can do easily is be wrong, and that's hardly worth the effort.

Milo. But . . . what bothers me is . . . well, why is it that even when things are correct, they don't really seem to be right?

Mathemagician. [*Grows sad and quiet.*] How true. It's been that way ever since Rhyme and Reason were banished. [*Sadness turns to fury.*] And all because of that stubborn wretch Azaz! It's all his fault.

Milo. Maybe if you discussed it with him . . .

Mathemagician. He's just too unreasonable! Why just last month, I sent him a very friendly letter, which he never had the courtesy to answer. See for yourself. [*Puts the letter on the easel. The letter reads:*]

4738 1919,

667 394107 5841 62589 85371 14

39588 7190434 203 27689 57131 481206.

5864 98053,

62179875073

Milo. But maybe he doesn't understand numbers.

Mathemagician. Nonsense! Everybody understands numbers. No matter what language you speak, they always mean the same thing. A seven is a seven everywhere in the world.

Milo. [*To* Tock *and* Humbug.] Everyone is so sensitive about what he knows best.

Tock. With your permission, sir, we'd like to rescue Rhyme and Reason.

Mathemagician. Has Azaz agreed to it?

Tock. Yes, sir.

Mathemagician. THEN I DON'T! Ever since they've been banished, we've never agreed on anything, and we never will.

Milo. Never?

Mathemagician. NEVER! And if you can prove otherwise, you have my permission to go.

Milo. Well then, with whatever Azaz agrees, you disagree.

Mathemagician. Correct.

Milo. And with whatever Azaz disagrees, you agree.

Mathemagician. [*Yawning, cleaning his nails.*] Also correct.

Milo. Then, each of you agrees that he will disagree with whatever each of you agrees with, and if you both disagree with the same thing, aren't you really in agreement?

TAKE NOTES

TAKE NOTES

Mathemagician. I'VE BEEN TRICKED! [*Figures it over, but comes up with the same answer.*]

Tock. And now may we go?

Mathemagician. [*Nods weakly.*] It's a long and dangerous journey. Long before you find them, the demons will know you're there. Watch out for them, because if you ever come face to face, it will be too late. But there is one other obstacle even more serious than that.

Milo. [*Terrified.*] What is it?

Mathemagician. I'm afraid I can't tell you until you return. But maybe I can give you something to help you out. [*Claps hands. ENTER the* Dodecahedron, *carrying something on a pillow. The* Mathemagician *takes it.*] Here is your own magic staff. Use it well and there is nothing it can't do for you. [*Puts a small, gleaming pencil in* Milo's *breast pocket.*]

Humbug. Are you sure you can't tell about that serious obstacle?

Mathemagician. Only when you return. And now the Dodecahedron will escort you to the road that leads to the Castle-in-the-Air. Farewell, my friends, and good luck to you. [*They shake hands, say goodbye, and the* Dodecahedron *leads them off.*] Good luck to you! [*To himself.*] Because you're sure going to need it. [*He watches them through a telescope and marks down the calculations.*]

Dodecahedron. [*He re-enters.*] Well, they're on their way.

Mathemagician. So I see... [Dodecahedron *stands waiting.*] Well, what is it?

Dodecahedron. I was just wondering myself, your Numbership. What actually is the serious obstacle you were talking about?

Mathemagician. [*Looks at him in surprise.*] You mean you really don't know?

BLACKOUT

Scene ii • The Land of Ignorance

TAKE NOTES

[*LIGHTS UP on* RHYME *and* REASON, *in their castle, looking out two windows.*]

RHYME. *I'm worried sick, I must confess*
I wonder if they'll have success
All the others tried in vain,
And were never seen or heard again.

REASON. Now, Rhyme, there's no need to be so pessimistic. Milo, Tock, and Humbug have just as much chance of succeeding as they do of failing.

RHYME. *But the demons are so deadly smart*
They'll stuff your brain and fill your heart
With petty thoughts and selfish dreams
And trap you with their nasty schemes.

REASON. Now, Rhyme, be reasonable, won't you? And calm down, you always talk in couplets when you get nervous. Milo has learned a lot from his journey. I think he's a match for the demons and that he might soon be knocking at our door. Now come on, cheer up, won't you?

RHYME. I'll try.

[*LIGHTS FADE on the* PRINCESSES *and COME UP on the little Car, traveling slowly.*]

MILO. So this is the Land of Ignorance. It's so dark. I can hardly see a thing. Maybe we should wait until morning.

VOICE. They'll be mourning for you soon enough. [*They look up and see a large, soiled, ugly bird with a dangerous beak and a malicious expression.*]

MILO. I don't think you understand. We're looking for a place to spend the night.

BIRD. [*Shrieking.*] It's not yours to spend!

MILO. That doesn't make any sense, you see . . .

BIRD. Dollars or cents, it's still not yours to spend.

MILO. But I don't mean . . .

BIRD. Of course you're mean. Anybody who'd spend a night that doesn't belong to him is very mean.

TOCK. Must you interrupt like that?

TAKE NOTES

Bird. Naturally, it's my job. I take the words right out of your mouth. Haven't we met before? I'm the Everpresent Wordsnatcher.

Milo. Are you a demon?

Bird. I'm afraid not. I've tried, but the best I can manage to be is a nuisance. [*Suddenly gets nervous as he looks beyond the three.*] And I don't have time to waste with you. [*Starts to leave.*]

Tock. What is it? What's the matter?

Milo. Hey, don't leave. I wanted to ask you some questions. . . . Wait!

Bird. Weight? Twenty-seven pounds. Bye-bye. [*Disappears.*]

Milo. Well, he was no help.

Man. Perhaps I can be of some assistance to you? [*There appears a beautifully dressed man, very polished and clean.*] Hello, little boy. [*Shakes* Milo's *hand.*] And how's the faithful dog? [*Pats* Tock.] And who is this handsome creature? [*Tips his hat to* Humbug.]

Humbug. [*To others.*] What a pleasant surprise to meet someone so nice in a place like this.

Man. But before I help you out, I wonder if first you could spare me a little of your time, and help me with a few small jobs?

Humbug. Why, certainly.

Tock. Gladly.

Milo. Sure, we'd be happy to.

Man. Splendid, for there are just three tasks. First, I would like to move this pile of sand from here to there. [*Indicates through pantomime a large pile of sand.*] But I'm afraid that all I have is this tiny tweezers. [*Hands it to* Milo, *who begins moving the sand one grain at a time.*] Second, I would like to empty this well and fill that other, but I have no bucket, so you'll have to use this eyedropper. [*Hands it to* Tock, *who begins to work.*] And finally, I must have a hole in this cliff, and here is a needle to dig it. [HUMBUG *eagerly begins. The man leans against a tree and stares vacantly off into space. The LIGHTS indicate the passage of time.*]

MILO. You know something? I've been working steadily for a long time, now, and I don't feel the least bit tired or hungry. I could go right on the same way forever.

MAN. Maybe you will. [*He yawns.*]

MILO. [*Whispers to* TOCK.] Well, I wish I knew how long it was going to take.

TOCK. Why don't you use your magic staff and find out?

MILO. [*Takes out pencil and calculates. To* MAN.] Pardon me, sir, but it's going to take 837 years to finish these jobs.

MAN. Is that so? What a shame. Well then you'd better get on with them.

MILO. But . . . it hardly seems worthwhile.

MAN. WORTHWHILE! Of course they're not worthwhile. I wouldn't ask you to do anything that was worthwhile.

TOCK. Then why bother?

MAN. Because, my friends, what could be more important than doing unimportant things? If you stop to do enough of them, you'll never get where you are going. [*Laughs villainously.*]

MILO. [*Gasps.*] Oh, no, you must be . . .

MAN. Quite correct! I am the Terrible Trivium, demon of petty tasks and worthless jobs, ogre of wasted effort and monster of habit. [*They start to back away from him.*] Don't try to leave, there's so much to do, and you still have 837 years to go on the first job.

MILO. But why do unimportant things?

MAN. Think of all the trouble it saves. If you spend all your time doing only the easy and useless jobs, you'll never have time to worry about the important

TAKE NOTES

TAKE NOTES

ones which are so difficult. [*Walks toward them whispering.*] Now do come and stay with me. We'll have such fun together. There are things to fill and things to empty, things to take away and things to bring back, things to pick up and things to put down . . . [*They are* transfixed *by his soothing voice. He is about to embrace them when a* VOICE *screams.*]

VOICE. Run! Run! [*They all wake up and run with the* TRIVIUM *behind. As the voice continues to call out directions, they follow until they lose the* TRIVIUM.] RUN! RUN! This way! This way! Over here! Over here! Up here! Down there! Quick, hurry up!

TOCK. [*Panting.*] I think we lost him.

VOICE. Keep going straight! Keep going straight! Now step up! Now step up!

MILO. Look out! [*They all fall into a Trap.*] But he said "up!"

VOICE. Well, I hope you didn't expect to get anywhere by listening to me.

HUMBUG. We're in a deep pit! We'll never get out of here.

VOICE. That is quite an accurate evaluation of the situation.

MILO. [*Shouting angrily.*] Then why did you help us at all?

VOICE. Oh, I'd do as much for anybody. Bad advice is my specialty. [*A Little Furry Creature appears.*] I'm the demon of Insincerity. I don't mean what I say; I don't mean what I do; and I don't mean what I am.

MILO. Then why don't you go away and leave us alone!

INSINCERITY. [VOICE] Now, there's no need to get angry. You're a very clever boy and I have complete confidence in you. You can certainly climb out of that pit . . . come on, try. . . .

MILO. I'm not listening to one word you say! You're just telling me what you think I'd like to hear, and not what is important.

INSINCERITY. Well, if that's the way you feel about it . . .

Milo. That's the way I feel about it. We will manage by ourselves without any unnecessary advice from you.

Insincerity. [*Stamping his foot.*] Well, all right for you! Most people listen to what I say, but if that's the way you feel, then I'll just go home. [*Exits in a huff.*]

Humbug. [*Who has been quivering with fright.*] And don't you ever come back! Well, I guess we showed him, didn't we?

Milo. You know something? This place is a lot more dangerous than I ever imagined.

Tock. [*Who's been surveying the situation.*] I think I figured a way to get out. Here, hop on my back. [Milo *does so.*] Now, you, Humbug, on top of Milo. [*He does so.*] Now hook your umbrella onto that tree and hold on. [*They climb over* Humbug, *then pull him up.*]

Humbug. [*As they climb.*] Watch it! Watch it, now. Ow, be careful of my back! My back! Easy, easy . . . oh, this is so difficult. Aren't you finished yet?

Tock. [*As he pulls up* Humbug.] There. Now, I'll lead for a while. Follow me, and we'll stay out of trouble. [*They walk and climb higher and higher.*]

Humbug. Can't we slow down a little?

Tock. Something tells me we better reach the Castle-in-the-Air as soon as possible, and not stop to rest for a single moment. [*They speed up.*]

Milo. What is it, Tock? Did you see something?

Tock. Just keep walking and don't look back.

Milo. You *did* see something!

Humbug. What is it? Another demon?

Tock. Not just one, I'm afraid. If you want to see what I'm talking about, then turn around. [*They turn around. The stage darkens and hundreds of Yellow Gleaming Eyes can be seen.*]

Humbug. Good grief! Do you see how many there are? Hundreds! The Overbearing Know-it-all, the Gross

TAKE NOTES

TAKE NOTES

Exaggeration, the Horrible Hopping Hindsight, . . . and look over there! The Triple Demons of Compromise! Let's get out of here! [*Starts to scurry.*] Hurry up, you two! Must you be so slow about everything?

Milo. Look! There it is, up ahead! The Castle-in-the-Air! [*They all run.*]

Humbug. They're gaining!

Milo. But there it is!

Humbug. I see it! I see it!

[*They reach the first step and are stopped by a little man in a frock coat, sleeping on a worn ledger. He has a long quill pen and a bottle of ink at his side. He is covered with ink stains over his clothes and wears spectacles.*]

Tock. Shh! Be very careful. [*They try to step over him, but he wakes up.*]

Senses Taker. [*From sleeping position.*] Names? [*He sits up.*]

Humbug. Well, I . . .

Senses Taker. *NAMES?* [*He opens book and begins to write, splattering himself with ink.*]

Humbug. Uh . . . Humbug, Tock and this is Milo.

Senses Taker. Splendid, splendid. I haven't had an "M" in ages.

Milo. What do you want our names for? We're sort of in a hurry.

Senses Taker. Oh, this won't take long. I'm the official Senses Taker and I must have some information before I can take your sense. Now if you'll just tell me: [*Handing them a form to fill. Speaking slowly and deliberately.*] When you were born, where you were born, why you were born, how old you are now, how old you were then, how old you'll be in a little while . . .

Milo. I wish he'd hurry up. At this rate, the demons will be here before we know it!

Senses Taker. . . . Your mother's name, your father's name, where you live, how long you've lived there, the schools you've attended, the schools you haven't attended . . .

Humbug. I'm getting writer's cramp.

Tock. I smell something very evil and it's getting stronger every second. [*To* Senses Taker.] May we go now?

Senses Taker. Just as soon as you tell me your height, your weight, the number of books you've read this year . . .

Milo. We have to go!

Senses Taker. All right, all right, I'll give you the short form. [*Pulls out a small piece of paper.*] Destination?

Milo. But we have to . . .

Senses Taker. *DESTINATION?*

Milo, Tock and **Humbug.** The Castle-in-the-Air! [*They throw down their papers and run past him up the first few stairs.*]

Senses Taker. Stop! I'm sure you'd rather see what I have to show you. [*Snaps his fingers; they freeze.*] A circus of your very own. [*CIRCUS MUSIC is heard.* Milo *seems to go into a trance.*] And wouldn't you enjoy this most wonderful smell? [Tock *sniffs and goes into a trance.*] And here's something I know you'll enjoy hearing . . . [*To* Humbug. *The sound of CHEERS and APPLAUSE for* Humbug *is heard, and he goes into a trance.*] There we are. And now, I'll just sit back and let the demons catch up with you.

[Milo *accidentally drops his package of gifts. The Package of Laughter from* Dr. Dischord *opens and the Sounds of Laughter are heard. After a moment,* Milo, Tock *and* Humbug *join in laughing and the spells are broken.*]

Milo. There was no circus.

Tock. There were no smells.

Humbug. The applause is gone.

Senses Taker. I warned you I was the Senses Taker. I'll steal your sense of Purpose, your sense of Duty, destroy your sense of Proportion—and but for one thing, you'd be helpless yet.

Milo. What's that?

TAKE NOTES

TAKE NOTES

Senses Taker. As long as you have the sound of laughter, I cannot take your sense of Humor. Agh! That horrible sense of humor.

Humbug. HERE THEY COME! LET'S GET OUT OF HERE!

[*The demons appear in nasty slithering hordes, running through the audience and up onto the stage, trying to attack* Tock, Milo *and* Humbug. *The three heroes run past the* Senses Taker *up the stairs toward the Castle-in-the-Air with the demons snarling behind them.*]

Milo. Don't look back! Just keep going! [*They reach the castle. The two* PRINCESSES *appear in the windows.*]

Princesses. Hurry! Hurry! We've been expecting you.

Milo. You must be the Princesses. We've come to rescue you.

Humbug. And the demons are close behind!

Tock. We should leave right away.

Princesses. We're ready anytime you are.

Milo. Good, now if you'll just come out. But wait a minute—there's no door! How can we rescue you from the Castle-in-the-Air if there's no way to get in or out?

Humbug. Hurry, Milo! They're gaining on us.

Reason. Take your time, Milo, and think about it.

Milo. Ummm, all right ... just give me a second or two. [*He thinks hard.*]

Humbug. I think I feel sick.

Milo. I've got it! Where's that package of presents? [*Opens the package of letters.*] Ah, here it is. [*Takes out the letters and sticks them on the door, spelling:*] E-N-T-R-A-N-C-E. Entrance. Now, let's see. [*Rummages through and spells in smaller letters:*] P-u-s-h. Push. [*He pushes and a door opens. The* PRINCESSES *come out of the castle. Slowly, the demons ascend the stairway.*]

Humbug. Oh, it's too late. They're coming up and there's no other way down!

Milo. Unless . . . [*Looks at* Tock.] Well . . . Time flies, doesn't it?

Tock. Quite often. Hold on, everyone, and I'll take you down.

Humbug. Can you carry us all?

Tock. We'll soon find out. Ready or not, here we go! [*His alarm begins to ring. They jump off the platform and disappear. The demons, howling with rage, reach the top and find no one there. They see the* PRINCESSES *and the heroes running across the stage and bound down the stairs after them and into the audience. There is a mad chase scene until they reach the stage again.*]

Humbug. I'm exhausted! I can't run another step.

Milo. We can't stop now. . . .

Tock. Milo! Look out there! [*The armies of* Azaz *and* Mathemagician *appear at the back of the theater, with the* KINGS *at their heads.*]

Azaz. [*As they march toward the stage.*] Don't worry, Milo, we'll take over now.

Mathemagician. Those demons may not know it, but their days are numbered!

Spelling Bee. Charge! C-H-A-R-G-E! Charge! [*They rush at the demons and battle until the demons run off howling. Everyone cheers. The* FIVE MINISTERS OF AZAZ *appear and shake* Milo's *hand.*]

Minister 1. Well done.

Minister 2. Fine job.

Minister 3. Good work!

Minister 4. Congratulations!

Minister 5. CHEERS! [*Everyone cheers again. A fanfare interrupts. A* Page *steps forward and reads from a large scroll:*]

Page. *Henceforth, and forthwith,*
Let it be known by one and all,
That Rhyme and Reason
Reign once more in Wisdom.

TAKE NOTES

TAKE NOTES

[*The* PRINCESSES *bow gratefully and kiss their brothers, the* KINGS.]

And furthermore,
The boy named Milo,
The dog known as Tock,
And the insect hereinafter referred to as the Humbug
Are hereby declared to be Heroes of the Realm.

[ALL *bow and salute the heroes.*]

MILO. But we never could have done it without a lot of help.

REASON. That may be true, but you had the courage to try, and what you can do is often a matter of what you *will* do.

AZAZ. That's why there was one very important thing about your quest we couldn't discuss until you returned.

MILO. I remember. What was it?

AZAZ. Very simple. It was impossible!

MATHEMAGICIAN. *Completely* impossible!

HUMBUG. Do you mean . . . ? [*Feeling faint.*] Oh . . . I think I need to sit down.

AZAZ. Yes, indeed, but if we'd told you then, you might not have gone.

MATHEMAGICIAN. And, as you discovered, many things are possible just as long as you don't know they're impossible.

MILO. I think I understand.

RHYME. I'm afraid it's time to go now.

REASON. And you must say goodbye.

MILO. To everyone? [*Looks around at the crowd. To* TOCK *and* HUMBUG.] Can't you two come with me?

HUMBUG. I'm afraid not, old man. I'd like to, but I've arranged for a lecture tour which will keep me occupied for years.

TOCK. And they do need a watchdog here.

Milo. Well, O.K., then. [Milo *hugs the* Humbug.]

Humbug. [*Sadly.*] Oh, bah.

Milo. [*He hugs* Tock, *and then faces everyone.*] Well, goodbye. We all spent so much time together, I know I'm going to miss you. [*To the* princesses.] I guess we would have reached you a lot sooner if I hadn't made so many mistakes.

Reason. You must never feel badly about making mistakes, Milo, as long as you take the trouble to learn from them. Very often you learn more by being wrong for the right reasons than you do by being right for the wrong ones.

Milo. But there's so much to learn.

Rhyme. That's true, but it's not just learning that's important. It's learning what to do with what you learn and learning why you learn things that matters.

Milo. I think I know what you mean, Princess. At least, I hope I do. [*The car is rolled forward and* Milo *climbs in.*] Goodbye! Goodbye! I'll be back someday! I will! Anyway, I'll try. [*As* Milo *drives the set of the Land of Ignorance begins to move offstage.*]

Azaz. Goodbye! Always remember. Words! Words! Words!

Mathemagician. And numbers!

Azaz. Now, don't tell me you think numbers are as important as words?

Mathemagician. Is that so? Why I'll have you know …
[*The set disappears, and* Milo's *Room is seen onstage.*]

Milo. [*As he drives on.*] Oh, oh, I hope they don't start all over again. Because I don't think I'll have much time in the near future to help them out. [*The sound of loud ticking is heard.* Milo *finds himself in his room. He gets out of the car and looks around.*]

The Clock. Did someone mention time?

Milo. Boy, I must have been gone for an awful long time. I wonder what time it is. [*Looks at clock.*]

TAKE NOTES

TAKE NOTES

Five o'clock. I wonder what day it is. [*Looks at calendar.*] It's still today! I've only been gone for an hour! [*He continues to look at his calendar, and then begins to look at his books and toys and maps and chemistry set with great interest.*]

Clock. An hour. Sixty minutes. How long it really lasts depends on what you do with it. For some people, an hour seems to last forever. For others, just a moment, and so full of things to do.

Milo. [*Looks at clock.*] Six o'clock already?

Clock. In an instant. In a trice. Before you have time to blink. [*The stage goes black in less than no time at all.*]

The Prince and the Pauper

adapted from a book by Mark Twain

TAKE NOTES

CHARACTERS

Edward, Prince of Wales	Justice
Tom Canty, *the Pauper*	Constable
Lord Hertford	Jailer
Lord St. John	Sir Hugh Hendon
King Henry VIII	Two Prisoners
Herald	Two Guards
Miles Hendon	Three Pages
John Canty, *Tom's father*	Lords and Ladies
Hugo, *a young thief*	Villagers
Two Women	

SCENE 1

TIME. *1547.*

SETTING. *Westminster Palace, England. Gates leading to courtyard are at right. Slightly to the left, off courtyard and inside gates, interior of palace anteroom is visible. There is a couch with a rich robe draped on it, screen at rear, bellcord, mirror, chairs, and a table with bowl of nuts, and a large golden seal on it. Piece of armor hangs on one wall. Exits are rear and downstage.*

AT RISE, TWO GUARDS—*One at right, one at left—stand in front of gates, and several* VILLAGERS *hover nearby, straining to see into courtyard where* PRINCE *may be seen through fence, playing.* TWO WOMEN *enter right.*

1ST WOMAN. I have walked all morning just to have a glimpse of Westminster Palace.

2ND WOMAN. Maybe if we can get near enough to the gates, we can have a glimpse of the young prince. *(*TOM CANTY, *dirty and ragged, comes out of crowd and steps close to gates.)* I have always dreamed of seeing a real prince! *(Excited, he presses his nose against gates.)*

1ST GUARD. Mind your manners, you young beggar! *(Seizes* TOM *by collar and sends him sprawling into*

TAKE NOTES

crowd. VILLAGERS *laugh, as* TOM *slowly gets to his feet.)*

PRINCE. *(Rushing to gates)* How dare you treat a poor subject of the King in such a manner! Open the gates and let him in! *(As* VILLAGERS *see* PRINCE, *they take off their hats and bow low.)*

VILLAGERS. *(Shouting together)* Long live the Prince of Wales! *(*GUARDS *open gates and* TOM *slowly passes through, as if in a dream.)*

PRINCE. *(To* TOM) You look tired, and you have been treated cruelly. I am Edward, Prince of Wales. What is your name?

TOM. *(Looking around in awe)* Tom Canty, Your Highness.

PRINCE. Come into the palace with me, Tom. *(*PRINCE *leads* TOM *into anteroom.* VILLAGERS *pantomime conversation, and all but a few exit.)* Where do you live, Tom?

TOM. In the city, Your Highness, in Offal[1] Court.

PRINCE. Offal Court? That is an odd name. Do you have parents?

TOM. Yes, Your Highness.

PRINCE. How does your father treat you?

TOM. If it please you, Your Highness, when I am not able to beg a penny for our supper, he treats me to beatings.

PRINCE. *(Shocked)* What! Beatings? My father is not a calm man, but he does not beat me. *(Looks at* TOM *thoughtfully)* You speak well and have an easy grace. Have you been schooled?

TOM. Very little, Your Highness. A good priest who shares our house in Offal Court has taught me from his books.

PRINCE. Do you have a pleasant life in Offal Court?

TOM. Pleasant enough, Your Highness, save when I am hungry. We have Punch and Judy shows,[2] and sometimes we lads have fights in the street.

---

1. **offal** (ô′ fəl) scraps left over when an animal is butchered.
2. **Punch and Judy shows** public puppet shows presented in Europe in the seventeenth century.

PRINCE. *(Eagerly)* I should like that. Tell me more.

TOM. In summer, we run races and swim in the river, and we love to wallow in the mud.

PRINCE. *(Sighing, wistfully)* If I could wear your clothes and play in the mud just once, with no one to forbid me, I think I could give up the crown!

TOM. *(Shaking his head)* And if I could wear your fine clothes just once, Your Highness . . .

PRINCE. Would you like that? Come, then. We shall change places. You can take off your rags and put on my clothes—and I will put on yours. *(He leads* TOM *behind screen, and they return shortly, each wearing the other's clothes.)* Let's look at ourselves in this mirror. *(Leads* TOM *to mirror)*

TOM. Oh, Your Highness, it is not proper for me to wear such clothes.

PRINCE. *(Excitedly, as he looks in mirror)* Heavens, do you not see it? We look like brothers! We have the same features and bearing. If we went about together, dressed alike, there is no one who could say which is the Prince of Wales and which Tom Canty!

TOM. *(Drawing back and rubbing his hand)* Your Highness, I am frightened. . . .

PRINCE. Do not worry. *(Seeing* TOM *rub his hand)* Is that a bruise on your hand?

TOM. Yes, but it is a slight thing, Your Highness.

PRINCE. *(Angrily)* It was shameful and cruel of that guard to strike you. Do not stir a step until I come back. I command you! *(He picks up golden Seal of England and carefully puts it into piece of armor. He then dashes out to gates.)* Open! Unbar the gates at once! *(*2ND GUARD *opens gates, and as* PRINCE *runs out, in rags,* 1ST GUARD *seizes him, boxes him on the ear, and knocks him to the ground.)*

1ST GUARD. Take that, you little beggar, for the trouble you have made for me with the Prince. *(*VILLAGERS *roar with laughter.)*

PRINCE. *(Picking himself up, turning on* GUARD *furiously)* I am Prince of Wales! You shall hang for laying your hand on me!

TAKE NOTES

TAKE NOTES

1ST GUARD. *(Presenting arms; mockingly)* I salute Your Gracious Highness! *(Then, angrily,* 1ST GUARD *shoves* PRINCE *roughly aside.)* Be off, you mad bag of rags! *(*PRINCE *is surrounded by* VILLAGERS, *who hustle him off.)*

VILLAGERS. *(Ad lib, as they exit, shouting)* Make way for His Royal Highness! Make way for the Prince of Wales! Hail to the Prince! *(Etc.)*

TOM. *(Admiring himself in mirror)* If only the boys in Offal Court could see me! They will not believe me when I tell them about this. *(Looks around anxiously)* But where is the Prince? *(Looks cautiously into courtyard.* TWO GUARDS *immediately snap to attention and salute. He quickly ducks back into anteroom as* HERTFORD *and* ST. JOHN *enter at rear.)*

HERTFORD. *(Going toward* TOM, *then stopping and bowing low)* My Lord, you look distressed. What is wrong?

TOM. *(Trembling)* Oh, I beg of you, be merciful. I am no Prince, but poor Tom Canty of Offal Court. Please let me see the Prince, and he will give my rags back to me and let me go unhurt. *(Kneeling)* Please, be merciful and spare me!

HERTFORD. *(Puzzled and disturbed)* Your Highness, on your knees? To me? *(Bows quickly, then, aside to* ST. JOHN*)* The Prince has gone mad! We must inform the King. *(To* TOM*)* A moment, Your Highness. *(*HERTFORD *and* ST. JOHN *exit rear.)*

TOM. Oh, there is no hope for me now. They will hang me for certain! *(*HERTFORD *and* ST. JOHN *re-enter, supporting* KING. TOM *watches in awe as they help him to couch, where he sinks down wearily.)*

KING. *(Beckoning* TOM *close to him)* Now, my son, Edward, my prince. What is this? Do you mean to deceive me, the King, your father, who loves you and treats you so kindly?

TOM. *(Dropping to his knees)* You are the King? Then I have no hope!

KING. *(Stunned)* My child, you are not well. Do not break your father's old heart. Say you know me.

TOM. Yes, you are my lord the King, whom God preserve.

KING. True, that is right. Now, you will not deny that you are Prince of Wales, as they say you did just a while ago?

TOM. I beg you, Your Grace, believe me. I am the lowest of your subjects, being born a pauper, and it is by a great mistake that I am here. I am too young to die. Oh, please, spare me, sire!

KING. *(Amazed)* Die? Do not talk so, my child. You shall not die.

TOM. *(Gratefully)* God save you, my king! And now, may I go?

KING. Go? Where would you go?

TOM. Back to the alley where I was born and bred to misery.

KING. My poor child, rest your head here. *(He holds* TOM'S *head and pats his shoulder, then turns to* HERTFORD *and* ST. JOHN.*)* Alas, I am old and ill, and my son is mad. But this shall pass. Mad or sane, he is my heir and shall rule England. Tomorrow he shall be installed and confirmed in his princely dignity! Bring the Great Seal!

HERTFORD. *(Bowing low)* Please, Your Majesty, you took the Great Seal from the Chancellor two days ago to give to His Highness the Prince.

KING. So I did. *(To* TOM*)* My child, tell me, where is the Great Seal?

TOM. *(Trembling)* Indeed, my lord, I do not know.

KING. Ah, your affliction hangs heavily upon you. 'Tis no matter. You will remember later. Listen, carefully! *(Gently, but firmly)* I command you to hide your affliction in all ways that be within your power. You shall deny to no one that you are the true prince, and if your memory should fail you upon any occasion of state, you shall be advised by your uncle, the Lord Hertford.

TOM. *(Resigned)* The King has spoken. The King shall be obeyed.

KING. And now, my child, I go to rest. *(He stands weakly, and* HERTFORD *leads him off, rear.)*

TAKE NOTES

TAKE NOTES

TOM. *(Wearily, to* ST. JOHN*)* May it please your lordship to let me rest now?

ST. JOHN. So it please Your Highness, it is for you to command and us to obey. But it is wise that you rest, for this evening you must attend the Lord Mayor's banquet in your honor. *(He pulls bellcord, and* THREE PAGES *enter and kneel before* TOM.*)*

TOM. Banquet? *(Terrified, he sits on couch and reaches for cup of water, but* 1ST PAGE *instantly seizes cup, drops on one knee, and serves it to him.* TOM *starts to take off his boots, but* 2ND PAGE *stops him and does it for him. He tries to remove his cape and gloves, and* 3RD PAGE *does it for him.)* I wonder that you do not try to breathe for me also! *(Lies down cautiously.* PAGES *cover him with robe, then back away and exit.)*

ST. JOHN. *(To* HERTFORD, *as he enters)* Plainly, what do you think?

HERTFORD. Plainly, this. The King is near death, my nephew the Prince of Wales is clearly mad and will mount the throne mad. God protect England, for she will need it!

ST. JOHN. Does it not seem strange that madness could so change his manner from what it used to be? It troubles me, his saying he is not the Prince.

HERTFORD. Peace, my lord! If he were an impostor and called himself Prince, that would be natural. But was there ever an impostor, who being called Prince by the King and court, denied it? Never! This is the true Prince gone mad. And tonight all London shall honor him. *(*HERTFORD *and* ST. JOHN *exit.* TOM *sits up, looks around helplessly, then gets up.)*

TOM. I should have thought to order something to eat. *(Sees bowl of nuts on table)* Ah! Here are some nuts! *(Looks around, sees Great Seal in armor, takes it out, looks at it curiously.)* This will make a good nutcracker. *(He takes bowl of nuts, sits on couch and begins to crack nuts with Great Seal and eat them, as curtain falls.)*

SCENE 2

TIME. *Later that night.*

SETTING. *A street in London, near Offal Court. Played before the curtain.*

AT RISE. PRINCE *limps in, dirty and tousled. He looks around wearily. Several* VILLAGERS *pass by, pushing against him.*

PRINCE. I have never seen this poor section of London. I must be near Offal Court. If I can only find it before I drop! *(*JOHN CANTY *steps out of crowd, seizes* PRINCE *roughly.)*

CANTY. Out at this time of night, and I warrant you haven't brought a farthing home! If that is the case and I do not break all the bones in your miserable body, then I am not John Canty!

PRINCE. *(Eagerly)* Oh, are you his father?

CANTY. *His* father? I am *your* father, and—

PRINCE. Take me to the palace at once, and your son will be returned to you. The King, my father, will make you rich beyond your wildest dreams. Oh, save me, for I am indeed the Prince of Wales.

CANTY. *(Staring in amazement)* Gone stark mad! But mad or not, I'll soon find where the soft places lie in your bones. Come home! *(Starts to drag* PRINCE *off)*

PRINCE. *(Struggling)* Let me go! I am the Prince of Wales, and the King shall have your life for this!

CANTY. *(Angrily)* I'll take no more of your madness! *(Raises stick to strike, but* PRINCE *struggles free and runs off, and* CANTY *runs after him)*

SCENE 3

SETTING. *Same as Scene 1, with addition of dining table, set with dishes and goblets, on raised platform. Throne-like chair is at head of table.*

AT RISE. *A banquet is in progress.* TOM, *in royal robes, sits at head of table, with* HERTFORD *at his right and* ST. JOHN *at his left.* LORDS *and* LADIES *sit around table eating and talking softly.*

TOM. *(To* HERTFORD*)* What is this, my Lord? *(Holds up a plate)*

TAKE NOTES

TAKE NOTES

HERTFORD. Lettuce and turnips, Your Highness.

TOM. Lettuce and turnips? I have never seen them before. Am I to eat them?

HERTFORD. *(Discreetly)* Yes, Your Highness, if you so desire. *(*TOM *begins to eat food with his fingers. Fanfare of trumpets is heard, and* HERALD *enters, carrying scroll. All turn to look.)*

HERALD. *(Reading from scroll)* His Majesty, King Henry VIII, is dead! The King is dead! *(All rise and return to* TOM, *who sits, stunned.)*

ALL. *(Together)* The King is dead. Long live the King! Long live Edward, King of England! *(All bow to* TOM. HERALD *bows and exits.)*

HERTFORD. *(To* TOM*)* Your Majesty, we must call the council. Come, St. John. *(*HERTFORD *and* ST. JOHN *lead* TOM *off at rear.* LORDS *and* LADIES *follow, talking among themselves. At gates, down right,* VILLAGERS *enter and mill about.* PRINCE *enters right, pounds on gates and shouts.)*

PRINCE. Open the gates! I am the Prince of Wales! Open, I say! And though I am friendless with no one to help me, I will not be driven from my ground.

MILES HENDON. *(Entering through crowd)* Though you be Prince or not, you are indeed a gallant lad and not friendless. Here I stand to prove it, and you might have a worse friend than Miles Hendon.

1ST VILLAGER. 'Tis another prince in disguise. Take the lad and dunk him in the pond! *(He seizes* PRINCE, *but* MILES *strikes him with the flat of his sword. Crowd, now angry, presses forward threateningly, when fanfare of trumpets is heard off-stage.* HERALD, *carrying scroll, enters up left at gates.)*

HERALD. Make way for the King's messenger! *(Reading from scroll)* His Majesty, King Henry VIII is dead! The King is dead! *(He exits right, repeating message, and* VILLAGERS *stand in stunned silence.)*

PRINCE. *(Stunned)* The King is dead!

1ST VILLAGER. *(Shouting)* Long live Edward, King of England!

VILLAGERS. *(Together)* Long live the King! *(Shouting, ad lib)* Long live King Edward! Heaven protect Edward, King of England! *(Etc.)*

MILES. *(Taking* PRINCE *by the arm)* Come, lad, before the crowd remembers us. I have a room at the inn, and you can stay there. *(He hurries off with stunned* PRINCE. TOM, *led by* HERTFORD, *enters courtyard up rear.* VILLAGERS *see them.)*

VILLAGERS. *(Together)* Long live the King! *(They fall to their knees as curtains close.)*

SCENE 4

SETTING. *Miles's room at the inn. At right is table set with dishes and bowls of food, a chair at each side. At left is bed, with table and chair next to it, and a window. Candle is on table.*

AT RISE. MILES *and* PRINCE *approach table.*

MILES. I have had a hot supper prepared. I'll bet you're hungry, lad.

PRINCE. Yes, I am. It's kind of you to let me stay with you, Miles. I am truly Edward, King of England, and you shall not go unrewarded. *(Sits at table)*

MILES. *(To himself)* First he called himself Prince, and now he is King. Well, I will humor him. *(Starts to sit)*

Prince. *(Angrily)* Stop! Would you sit in the presence of the King?

Miles. *(Surprised, standing up quickly)* I beg your pardon, Your Majesty. I was not thinking. *(Stares uncertainly at* PRINCE, *who sits at table, expectantly.* MILES *starts to uncover dishes of food, serves* PRINCE *and fills glasses.)*

PRINCE. Miles, you have a gallant way about you. Are you nobly born?

MILES. My father is a baronet,[3] Your Majesty.

PRINCE. Then you must also be a baronet.

MILES. *(Shaking his head)* My father banished me from home seven years ago, so I fought in the wars. I was taken prisoner, and I have spent the past seven years in prison. Now I am free, and I am returning home.

PRINCE. You have been shamefully wronged! But I will make things right for you. You have saved me from

3. baronet a member of the British upper class.

TAKE NOTES

TAKE NOTES

injury and possible death. Name your reward and if it be within the compass of my royal power, it is yours.

MILES. *(Pausing briefly, then dropping to his knee)* Since Your Majesty is pleased to hold my simple duty worthy of reward, I ask that I and my successors may hold the privilege of sitting in the presence of the King.

PRINCE. *(Taking* MILES'S *sword, tapping him lightly on each shoulder)* Rise and seat yourself. *(Returns sword to* MILES, *then rises and goes over to bed)*

MILES. *(Rising)* He should have been born a king. He plays the part to a marvel! If I had not thought of this favor, I might have had to stand for weeks. *(Sits down and begins to eat)*

PRINCE. Sir Miles, you will stand guard while I sleep. *(Lies down and instantly falls asleep)*

MILES. Yes, Your Majesty. *(With a rueful look at his uneaten supper, he stands up.)* Poor little chap. I suppose his mind has been disordered with ill usage. *(Covers* PRINCE *with his cape)* Well, I will be his friend and watch over him. *(Blows out candle, then yawns, sits on chair next to bed, and falls asleep.* JOHN CANTY *and* HUGO *appear at window, peer around room, then enter cautiously through window. They lift the sleeping* PRINCE, *staring nervously at* MILES.*)*

CANTY. *(In loud whisper)* I swore the day he was born he would be a thief and a beggar, and I won't lose him now. Lead the way to the camp, Hugo! *(*CANTY *and* HUGO *carry* PRINCE *off right, as* MILES *sleeps on and curtain falls.)*

SCENE 5

TIME. *Two weeks later.*

SETTING. *Country village street.*

BEFORE RISE. VILLAGERS *walk about.* CANTY, HUGO, *and* PRINCE *enter.*

CANTY. I will go in this direction. Hugo, keep my mad son with you, and see that he doesn't escape again! *(Exits)*

TAKE NOTES

HUGO. *(Seizing* PRINCE *by the arm)* He won't escape! I'll see that he earns his bread today, or else!

PRINCE. *(Pulling away)* I will not beg with you, and I will not steal! I have suffered enough in this miserable company of thieves!

HUGO. You shall suffer more if you do not do as I tell you! *(Raises clenched fist at* PRINCE*)* Refuse if you dare! *(*WOMAN *enters, carrying wrapped bundle in a basket on her arm.)* Wait here until I come back. *(*HUGO *sneaks along after* WOMAN, *then snatches her bundle, runs back to* PRINCE, *and thrusts it into his arms.)* Run after me and call, "Stop, thief!" But be sure you lead her astray! *(Runs off.* PRINCE *throws down bundle in disgust.)*

WOMAN. Help! Thief! Stop, thief! *(Rushes at* PRINCE *and seizes him, just as several* VILLAGERS *enter)* You little thief! What do you mean by robbing a poor woman? Somebody bring the constable! *(*MILES *enters and watches.)*

1ST VILLAGER. *(Grabbing* PRINCE*)* I'll teach him a lesson, the little villain!

PRINCE. *(Struggling)* Take your hands off me! I did not rob this woman!

MILES. *(Stepping out of crowd and pushing man back with the flat of his sword)* Let us proceed gently, my friends. This is a matter for the law.

PRINCE. *(Springing to* MILES'S *side)* You have come just in time, Sir Miles. Carve this rabble to rags!

MILES. Speak softly. Trust in me and all shall go well.

CONSTABLE. *(Entering and reaching for* PRINCE*)* Come along, young rascal!

MILES. Gently, good friend. He shall go peaceably to the Justice.

PRINCE. I will not go before a Justice! I did not do this thing!

MILES. *(Taking him aside)* Sire, will you reject the laws of the realm, yet demand that your subjects respect them?

PRINCE. *(Calmer)* You are right, Sir Miles. Whatever the King requires a subject to suffer under the law,

TAKE NOTES

he will suffer himself while he holds the station of a subject. *(CONSTABLE leads them off right. VILLAGERS follow. Curtain)*

* * * * *

SETTING. *Office of the* JUSTICE. *A high bench is at center.*

AT RISE. JUSTICE *sits behind bench.* CONSTABLE *enters with* MILES *and* PRINCE, *followed by* VILLAGERS. WOMAN *carries wrapped bundle.*

CONSTABLE. *(To* JUSTICE*)* A young thief, your worship, is accused of stealing a dressed pig from this poor woman.

JUSTICE. *(Looking down at* PRINCE, *then* WOMAN*)* My good woman, are you absolutely certain this lad stole your pig?

WOMAN. It was none other than he, your worship.

JUSTICE. Are there no witnesses to the contrary? *(All shake their heads.)* Then the lad stands convicted. *(To* WOMAN*)* What do you hold this property to be worth?

WOMAN. Three shillings and eight pence, your worship.

JUSTICE. *(Leaning down to* WOMAN*)* Good woman, do you know that when one steals a thing above the value of thirteen pence, the law says he shall hang for it?

WOMAN. *(Upset)* Oh, what have I done? I would not hang the poor boy for the whole world! Save me from this, your worship. What can I do?

JUSTICE. *(Gravely)* You may revise the value, since it is not yet written in the record.

WOMAN. Then call the pig eight pence, your worship.

JUSTICE. So be it. You may take your property and go. *(*WOMAN *starts off, and is followed by* CONSTABLE. MILES *follows them cautiously down right.)*

CONSTABLE. *(Stopping* WOMAN*)* Good woman, I will buy your pig from you. *(Takes coins from pocket)* Here is eight pence.

WOMAN. Eight pence! It cost me three shillings and eight pence!

CONSTABLE. Indeed! Then come back before his worship and answer for this. The lad must hang!

WOMAN. No! No! Say no more. Give me the eight pence and hold your peace. *(*CONSTABLE *hands her coins and takes pig.* WOMAN *exits, angrily.* MILES *returns to bench.)*

JUSTICE. The boy is sentenced to a fortnight in the common jail. Take him away, Constable! *(*JUSTICE *exits.* PRINCE *gives* MILES *a nervous glance.)*

MILES. *(Following* CONSTABLE*)* Good sir, turn your back a moment and let the poor lad escape. He is innocent.

CONSTABLE. *(Outraged)* What? You say this to me? Sir, I arrest you in—

MILES. Do not be so hasty! *(Slyly)* The pig you have purchased for eight pence may cost you your neck, man.

CONSTABLE. *(Laughing nervously)* Ah, but I was merely jesting with the woman, sir.

MILES. Would the Justice think it a jest?

CONSTABLE. Good sir! The Justice has no more sympathy with a jest than a dead corpse! *(Perplexed)* Very well, I will turn my back and see nothing! But go quickly! *(Exits)*

MILES. *(To* PRINCE*)* Come, my liege. We are free to go. And that band of thieves shall not set hands on you again, I swear it!

PRINCE. *(Wearily)* Can you believe, Sir Miles, that in the last fortnight, I, the King of England, have escaped from thieves and begged for food on the road? I have slept in a barn with a calf! I have washed dishes in a peasant's kitchen, and narrowly escaped death. And not once in all of my wanderings did I see a courier searching for me! Is it no matter for commotion and distress that the head of state is gone?

MILES. *(Sadly, aside)* Still busy with his pathetic dream. *(To* PRINCE*)* It is strange indeed my liege. But come, I will take you to my father's home in Kent. We are not far away. There you may rest in a house with seventy rooms! Come, I am all impatience to be home again! *(They exit,* MILES *in cheerful spirits,* PRINCE *looking puzzled, as curtains close.)*

TAKE NOTES

TAKE NOTES

SCENE 6

SETTING. *Village jail. Bare stage, with barred window on one wall.*

AT RISE. TWO PRISONERS, *in chains, are onstage.* JAILER *shoves* MILES *and* PRINCE, *in chains, onstage. They struggle and protest.*

MILES. But I tell you I *am* Miles Hendon! My brother, Sir Hugh, has stolen my bride and my estate!

JAILER. Be silent! Impostor! Sir Hugh will see that you pay well for claiming to be his dead brother and for assaulting him in his own house! *(Exits)*

MILES. *(Sitting, with head in hands)* Oh, my dear Edith . . . now wife to my brother Hugh, against her will, and my poor father . . . dead!

1ST PRISONER. At least you have your life, sir. I am sentenced to be hanged for killing a deer in the King's park.

2ND PRISONER. And I must hang for stealing a yard of cloth to dress my children.

PRINCE. *(Moved; to* PRISONERS*)* When I mount my throne, you shall all be free. And the laws that have dishonored you shall be swept from the books. *(Turning away)* Kings should go to school to learn their own laws and be merciful.

1ST PRISONER. What does the lad mean? I have heard that the King is mad, but merciful.

2ND PRISONER. He is to be crowned at Westminster[4] tomorrow.

PRINCE. *(Violently)* King? What King, good sir?

1ST PRISONER. Why, we have only one, his most sacred majesty, King Edward the Sixth.

2ND PRISONER. And whether he be mad or not, his praises are on all men's lips. He has saved many innocent lives, and now he means to destroy the cruelest laws that oppress the people.

PRINCE. *(Turning away, shaking his head)* How can this be? Surely it is not that little beggar boy! *(*SIR HUGH *enters with* JAILER.*)*

---

4. **Westminster** Westminster Abbey, church in London that hosts coronations and other important ceremonies.

SIR HUGH. Seize the impostor!

MILES. *(As* JAILER *pulls him to his feet)* Hugh, this has gone far enough!

SIR HUGH. You will sit in the public stocks for two hours, and the boy would join you if he were not so young. See to it, jailer, and after two hours, you may release them. Meanwhile, I ride to London for the coronation! *(*SIR HUGH *exits and* MILES *is hustled out by* JAILER.*)*

PRINCE. Coronation! What does he mean? There can be no coronation without me! *(Curtain falls.)*

SCENE 7

TIME. *Coronation Day.*

SETTING. *Outside gates of Westminster Abbey, played before curtain. Painted screen or flat at rear represents Abbey. Throne is center. Bench is near it.*

AT RISE. LORDS *and* LADIES *crowd Abbey. Outside gates,* GUARDS *drive back cheering* VILLAGERS, *among them* MILES.

MILES. *(Distraught)* I've lost him! Poor little chap! He has been swallowed up in the crowd! *(Fanfare of trumpets is heard, then silence.* HERTFORD, ST. JOHN, LORDS *and* LADIES *enter slowly, in a procession followed by* PAGES, *one of whom carries crown on small cushion.* TOM *follows procession, looking about nervously. Suddenly,* PRINCE, *in rags, steps out from crowd, his hand raised.)*

PRINCE. I forbid you to set the crown of England upon that head. I am the King!

HERTFORD. Seize the little vagabond!

TOM. I forbid it! He *is* the King! *(Kneels before* PRINCE*)* Oh, my lord the King, let poor Tom Canty be the first to say, "Put on your crown and enter into your own right again." *(*HERTFORD *and several* LORDS *look closely at both boys.)*

HERTFORD. This is strange indeed. *(To* TOM*)* By your favor, sir, I wish to ask certain questions of this lad.

PRINCE. I will answer truly whatever you may ask, my lord.

TAKE NOTES

TAKE NOTES

HERTFORD. But if you have been well trained, you may answer my questions as well as our lord the King. I need a definite proof. *(Thinks a moment)* Ah! Where lies the Great Seal of England? It has been missing for weeks, and only the true Prince of Wales can say where it lies.

TOM. Wait! Was the seal round and thick, with letters engraved on it? *(*HERTFORD *nods.)* I know where it is, but it was not I who put it there. The rightful King shall tell you. *(To* PRINCE*)* Think, my King, it was the very last thing you did that day before you rushed out of the palace wearing my rags.

PRINCE. *(Pausing)* I recall how we exchanged clothes, but have no recollection of hiding the Great Seal.

TOM. *(Eagerly)* Remember when you saw the bruise on my hand, you ran to the door, but first you hid this thing you call the Seal.

PRINCE. *(Suddenly)* Ah! I remember! *(To* ST. JOHN*)* Go, my good St. John, and you will find the Great Seal in the armor that hangs on the wall in my chamber. *(*ST. JOHN *hesitates, but at a nod from* TOM, *hurries off.)*

TOM. *(Pleased)* Right, my King! Now the scepter of England is yours again. *(*ST. JOHN *returns in a moment with Great Seal.)*

ALL. *(Shouting)* Long live Edward, King of England! *(*TOM *takes off his cape and throws it over* PRINCE'S *rags. Trumpet fanfare is heard.* ST. JOHN *takes crown and places it on* PRINCE. *All kneel.)*

HERTFORD. Let the small impostor be flung into the Tower![5]

PRINCE. *(Firmly)* I will not have it so. But for him, I would not have my crown. *(To* TOM*)* My poor boy, how was it that you could remember where I hid the Seal, when I could not?

TOM. *(Embarrassed)* I did not know what it was, my King, and I used it to . . . to crack nuts. *(All laugh, and* TOM *steps back.* MILES *steps forward, staring in amazement.)*

MILES. Is he really the King? Is he indeed the sovereign of England, and not the poor and

5. **Tower** the Tower of London, site of a prison and place of execution.

friendless Tom o' Bedlam[6] I thought he was? *(He sinks down on bench.)* I wish I had a bag to hide my head in!

1ST GUARD. *(Rushing up to him)* Stand up, you mannerless clown! How dare you sit in the presence of the King!

PRINCE. Do not touch him! He is my trusty servant, Miles Hendon, who saved me from shame and possible death. For his service, he owns the right to sit in my presence.

MILES. *(Bowing, then kneeling)* Your Majesty!

PRINCE. Rise, Sir Miles. I command that Sir Hugh Hendon, who sits within this hall, be seized and put under lock and key until I have need of him. *(Beckons to* TOM*)* From what I have heard, Tom Canty, you have governed the realm with royal gentleness and mercy in my absence. Henceforth, you shall hold the honorable title of King's Ward! *(*TOM *kneels and kisses* PRINCE'S *hand.)* And because I have suffered with the poorest of my subjects and felt the cruel force of unjust laws, I pledge myself to a reign of mercy for all! *(All bow low, then rise.)*

ALL. *(Shouting)* Long live the King! Long live Edward, King of England! *(Curtain)*

THE END

---

6. Bedlam British asylum for the mentally ill.

TAKE NOTES

TAKE NOTES

Black Cowboy, Wild Horses: A True Story

by Julius Lester

First Light. Bob Lemmons rode his horse slowly up the rise. When he reached the top, he stopped at the edge of the bluff. He looked down at the corral where the other cowboys were beginning the morning chores, then turned away and stared at the land stretching as wide as love in every direction. The sky was curved as if it were a lap on which the earth lay napping like a curled cat. High above, a hawk was suspended on cold threads of unseen winds. Far, far away, at what looked to be the edge of the world, land and sky kissed.

He guided Warrior, his black stallion, slowly down the bluff. When they reached the bottom, the horse reared, eager to run across the vastness of the plains until he reached forever. Bob smiled and patted him gently on the neck. "Easy. Easy," he whispered. "We'll have time for that. But not yet."

He let the horse trot for a while, then slowed him and began peering intently at the ground as if looking for the answer to a question he scarcely understood.

It was late afternoon when he saw them—the hoofprints of mustangs, the wild horses that lived on the plains. He stopped, dismounted, and walked around carefully until he had seen all the prints. Then he got down on his hands and knees to examine them more closely.

Some people learned from books. Bob had been a slave and never learned to read words. But he could look at the ground and read what animals had walked on it, their size and weight, when they had passed by, and where they were going. No one he knew could bring in mustangs by themselves, but Bob could make horses think he was one of them—because he was.

He stood, reached into his saddlebag, took out an apple, and gave it to Warrior, who chewed with noisy enthusiasm. It was a herd of eight mares, a colt, and a stallion. They had passed there two days ago. He would see them soon. But he needed to smell of sun, moon, stars, and wind before the mustangs would accept him.

The sun went down and the chilly night air came quickly. Bob took the saddle, saddlebag, and blanket off Warrior. He was cold, but could not make a fire. The mustangs would smell the smoke in his clothes from miles away. He draped a thick blanket around himself, then took the cotton sack of dried fruit, beef jerky, and nuts from his saddlebag and ate. When he was done, he lay his head on his saddle and was quickly asleep. Warrior grazed in the tall, sweet grasses.

As soon as the sun's round shoulders came over the horizon, Bob awoke. He ate, filled his canteen, and saddling Warrior, rode away. All day he followed the tracks without hurrying.

Near dusk, clouds appeared, piled atop each other like mountains made of fear. Lightning flickered from within them like candle flames shivering in a breeze. Bob heard the faint but distinct rumbling of thunder. Suddenly lightning vaulted from cloud to cloud across the curved heavens.

Warrior reared, his front hooves pawing as if trying to knock the white streaks of fire from the night sky. Bob raced Warrior to a nearby ravine as the sky exploded sheets of light. And there, in the distance, beneath the ghostly light, Bob saw the herd of mustangs. As if sensing their presence, Warrior rose into the air once again, this time not challenging the heavens but almost in greeting. Bob thought he saw the mustang stallion rise in response as the earth shuddered from the sound of thunder.

Then the rain came as hard and stinging as remorse. Quickly Bob put on his poncho, and turning Warrior away from the wind and the rain, waited. The storm would pass soon. Or it wouldn't. There was nothing to do but wait.

Finally the rain slowed and then stopped. The clouds thinned, and there, high in the sky, the moon appeared as white as grief. Bob slept in the saddle while Warrior grazed on the wet grasses.

TAKE NOTES

TAKE NOTES

The sun rose into a clear sky and Bob was awake immediately. The storm would have washed away the tracks, but they had been going toward the big river. He would go there and wait.

By mid-afternoon he could see the ribbon of river shining in the distance. He stopped, needing only to be close enough to see the horses when they came to drink. Toward evening he saw a trail of rolling, dusty clouds.

In front was the mustang herd. As it reached the water, the stallion slowed and stopped. He looked around, his head raised, nostrils flared, smelling the air. He turned in Bob's direction and sniffed the air again.

Bob tensed. Had he come too close too soon? If the stallion smelled anything new, he and the herd would be gone and Bob would never find them again. The stallion seemed to be looking directly at him. Bob was too far away to be seen, but he did not even blink his eyes, afraid the stallion would hear the sound. Finally the stallion began drinking and the other horses followed. Bob let his breath out slowly. He had been accepted.

The next morning he crossed the river and picked up the herd's trail. He moved Warrior slowly, without sound, without dust. Soon he saw them grazing. He stopped. The horses did not notice him. After a while he moved forward, slowly, quietly. The stallion raised his head. Bob stopped.

When the stallion went back to grazing, Bob moved forward again. All day Bob watched the herd, moving only when it moved but always coming closer. The mustangs sensed his presence. They thought he was a horse. So did he.

The following morning Bob and Warrior walked into the herd. The stallion eyed them for a moment. Then, as if to test this newcomer, he led the herd off in a gallop. Bob lay flat across Warrior's back and moved with the herd. If anyone had been watching, they would not have noticed a man among the horses.

When the herd set out early the next day, it was moving slowly. If the horses had been going faster, it would not have happened.

The colt fell to the ground as if she had stepped into a hole and broken her leg. Bob and the horses heard the chilling sound of the rattles. Rattlesnakes didn't always give a warning before they struck. Sometimes, when someone or something came too close, they bit with the fury of fear.

The horses whinnied and pranced nervously, smelling the snake and death among them. Bob saw the rattler, as beautiful as a necklace, sliding silently through the tall grasses. He made no move to kill it. Everything in nature had the right to protect itself, especially when it was afraid.

The stallion galloped to the colt. He pushed at her. The colt struggled to get up, but fell to her side, shivering and kicking feebly with her thin legs. Quickly she was dead.

Already vultures circled high in the sky. The mustangs milled aimlessly. The colt's mother whinnied, refusing to leave the side of her colt. The stallion wanted to move the herd from there, and pushed the mare with his head. She refused to budge, and he nipped her on the rump. She skittered away. Before she could return to the colt, the stallion bit her again, this time harder. She ran toward the herd. He bit her a third time, and the herd was off. As they galloped away, Bob looked back. The vultures were descending from the sky as gracefully as dusk.

It was time to take over the herd. The stallion would not have the heart to fight fiercely so soon after the death of the colt. Bob galloped Warrior to the front and wheeled around, forcing the stallion to stop quickly. The herd, confused, slowed and stopped also.

Bob raised Warrior to stand high on his back legs, fetlocks pawing and kicking the air. The stallion's eyes widened. He snorted and pawed the ground, surprised and uncertain. Bob charged at the stallion.

Both horses rose on hind legs, teeth bared as they kicked at each other. When they came down, Bob charged Warrior at the stallion again, pushing him backward. Bob rushed yet again.

The stallion neighed loudly, and nipped Warrior on the neck. Warrior snorted angrily, reared, and kicked out with his forelegs, striking the stallion on the nose.

TAKE NOTES

TAKE NOTES

Still maintaining his balance, Warrior struck again and again. The mustang stallion cried out in pain. Warrior pushed hard against the stallion. The stallion lost his footing and fell to the earth. Warrior rose, neighing triumphantly, his front legs pawing as if seeking for the rungs on which he could climb a ladder into the sky.

The mustang scrambled to his feet, beaten. He snorted weakly. When Warrior made as if to attack again, the stallion turned, whinnied weakly, and trotted away.

Bob was now the herd's leader, but would they follow him? He rode slowly at first, then faster and faster. The mustangs followed as if being led on ropes.

Throughout that day and the next he rode with the horses. For Bob there was only the bulging of the horses' dark eyes, the quivering of their flesh, the rippling of muscles and bending of bones in their bodies. He was now sky and plains and grass and river and horse.

When his food was almost gone, Bob led the horses on one last ride, a dark surge of flesh flashing across the plains like black lightning. Toward evening he led the herd up the steep hillside, onto the bluff, and down the slope toward the big corral. The cowboys heard him coming and opened the corral gate. Bob led the herd, but at the last moment he swerved Warrior aside, and the mustangs flowed into the fenced enclosure. The cowboys leaped and shouted as they quickly closed the gate.

Bob rode away from them and back up to the bluff. He stopped and stared out onto the plains. Warrior reared and whinnied loudly.

"I know," Bob whispered. "I know. Maybe someday."

Maybe someday they would ride with the mustangs, ride to that forever place where land and sky kissed, and then ride on. Maybe someday.

The Tiger Who Would Be King

by James Thurber

TAKE NOTES

One morning the tiger woke up in the jungle and told his mate that he was king of beasts.

"Leo, the lion, is king of beasts," she said.

"We need a change," said the tiger. "The creatures are crying for a change."

The tigress listened but she could hear no crying, except that of her cubs.

"I'll be king of beasts by the time the moon rises," said the tiger. "It will be a yellow moon with black stripes, in my honor."

"Oh, sure," said the tigress as she went to look after her young, one of whom, a male, very like his father, had got an imaginary thorn in his paw.

The tiger prowled through the jungle till he came to the lion's den. "Come out," he roared, "and greet the king of beasts! The king is dead, long live the king!"

Inside the den, the lioness woke her mate. "The king is here to see you," she said.

"What king?" he inquired, sleepily.

"The king of beasts," she said.

"I am the king of beasts," roared Leo, and he charged out of the den to defend his crown against the pretender.

It was a terrible fight, and it lasted until the setting of the sun. All the animals of the jungle joined in, some taking the side of the tiger and others the side of the lion. Every creature from the aardvark to the zebra took part in the struggle to overthrow the lion or to repulse the tiger, and some did not know which they were fighting for, and some fought for both, and some fought whoever was nearest, and some fought for the sake of fighting.

"What are we fighting for?" someone asked the aardvark.

"The old order," said the aardvark.

TAKE NOTES

"What are we dying for?" someone asked the zebra.

"The new order," said the zebra.

When the moon rose, fevered and gibbous,[1] it shone upon a jungle in which nothing stirred except a macaw[2] and a cockatoo,[3] screaming in horror. All the beasts were dead except the tiger, and his days were numbered and his time was ticking away. He was monarch of all he surveyed, but it didn't seem to mean anything.

---

1. **gibbous** (gib´ əs) *adj.* more than half but less than completely illuminated.
2. **macaw** (mə kô´) *n.* bright-colored, harsh-voiced parrot of Central or South America.
3. **cockatoo** (käk´ ə to͞o´) *n.* crested parrot with white feathers tinged with yellow or pink.

The Ant and the Dove

by Leo Tolstoy

TAKE NOTES

A thirsty ant went to the stream to drink. Suddenly it got caught in a whirlpool and was almost carried away.

At that moment a dove was passing by with a twig in its beak. The dove dropped the twig for the tiny insect to grab hold of. So it was that the ant was saved.

A few days later a hunter was about to catch the dove in his net. When the ant saw what was happening, it walked right up to the man and bit him on the foot. Startled, the man dropped the net. And the dove, thinking that you never can tell how or when a kindness may be repaid, flew away.

TAKE NOTES

Arachne

by Olivia E. Coolidge

Arachne [ə rak´ nē] was a maiden who became famous throughout Greece, though she was neither wellborn nor beautiful and came from no great city. She lived in an obscure little village, and her father was a humble dyer of wool.

In this he was very skillful, producing many varied shades, while above all he was famous for the clear, bright scarlet which is made from shellfish, and which was the most glorious of all the colors used in ancient Greece. Even more skillful than her father was Arachne. It was her task to spin the fleecy wool into a fine, soft thread and to weave it into cloth on the high, standing loom within the cottage. Arachne was small and pale from much working. Her eyes were light and her hair was a dusty brown, yet she was quick and graceful, and her fingers, roughened as they were, went so fast that it was hard to follow their flickering movements. So soft and even was her thread, so fine her cloth, so gorgeous her embroidery, that soon her products were known all over Greece. No one had ever seen the like of them before.

At last Arachne's fame became so great that people used to come from far and wide to watch her working. Even the graceful nymphs[1] would steal in from stream or forest and peep shyly through the dark doorway, watching in wonder the white arms of Arachne as she stood at the loom and threw the shuttle from hand to hand between the hanging threads, or drew out the long wool, fine as a hair, from the distaff[2] as she sat spinning. "Surely Athene[3] herself must have taught her," people would murmur to one another. "Who else could know the secret of such marvelous skill?"

1. **nymphs** (nimfs) *n.* minor nature goddesses, represented as beautiful maidens living in rivers, trees, and mountains.
2. **distaff** (dis´ taf) *n.* stick on which flax or wool is wound for spinning.
3. **Athene** (ə thē´ nē) *n.* Greek goddess of wisdom, skills, and warfare.

Arachne was used to being wondered at, and she was immensely proud of the skill that had brought so many to look on her. Praise was all she lived for, and it displeased her greatly that people should think anyone, even a goddess, could teach her anything. Therefore when she heard them murmur, she would stop her work and turn round indignantly to say, "With my own ten fingers I gained this skill, and by hard practice from early morning till night. I never had time to stand looking as you people do while another maiden worked. Nor if I had, would I give Athene credit because the girl was more skillful than I. As for Athene's weaving, how could there be finer cloth or more beautiful embroidery than mine? If Athene herself were to come down and compete with me, she could do no better than I." •

One day when Arachne turned round with such words, an old woman answered her, a gray old woman, bent and very poor, who stood leaning on a staff and peering at Arachne amid the crowd of onlookers. "Reckless girl," she said, "how dare you claim to be equal to the immortal gods themselves? I am an old woman and have seen much. Take my advice and ask pardon of Athene for your words. Rest content with your fame of being the best spinner and weaver that mortal eyes have ever beheld."

"Stupid old woman," said Arachne indignantly, "who gave you a right to speak in this way to me? It is easy to see that you were never good for anything in your day, or you would not come here in poverty and rags to gaze at my skill. If Athene resents my words, let her answer them herself. I have challenged her to a contest, but she, of course, will not come. It is easy for the gods to avoid matching their skill with that of men."

At these words the old woman threw down her staff and stood erect. The wondering onlookers saw her grow tall and fair and stand clad in long robes of dazzling white. They were terribly afraid as they realized that they stood in the presence of Athene. Arachne herself flushed red for a moment, for she had never really believed that the goddess would hear her. Before the group that was gathered there she would not give in;

TAKE NOTES

TAKE NOTES

so pressing her pale lips together in obstinacy and pride, she led the goddess to one of the great looms and set herself before the other. Without a word both began to thread the long woolen strands that hang from the rollers, and between which the shuttle[4] moves back and forth. Many skeins lay heaped beside them to use, bleached white, and gold, and scarlet, and other shades, varied as the rainbow. Arachne had never thought of giving credit for her success to her father's skill in dyeing, though in actual truth the colors were as remarkable as the cloth itself.

Soon there was no sound in the room but the breathing of the onlookers, the whirring of the shuttles, and the creaking of the wooden frames as each pressed the thread up into place or tightened the pegs by which the whole was held straight. The excited crowd in the doorway began to see that the skill of both in truth was very nearly equal, but that, however the cloth might turn out, the goddess was the quicker of the two. A pattern of many pictures was growing on her loom. There was a border of twined branches of the olive, Athene's favorite tree, while in the middle, figures began to appear. As they looked at the glowing colors, the spectators realized that Athene was weaving into her pattern a last warning to Arachne. The central figure was the goddess herself competing with Poseidon for possession of the city of Athens; but in the four corners were mortals who had tried to strive with gods and pictures of the awful fate that had overtaken them. The goddess ended a little before Arachne and stood back from her marvelous work to see what the maiden was doing.

Never before had Arachne been matched against anyone whose skill was equal, or even nearly equal to her own. As she stole glances from time to time at Athene and saw the goddess working swiftly, calmly, and always a little faster than herself, she became angry instead of frightened, and an evil thought came into her head. Thus as Athene stepped back a pace to watch Arachne finishing her work, she saw that the maiden had taken for her design a pattern of scenes which showed evil or unworthy actions of the

4. **shuttle** (shut′ əl) *n.* instrument used in weaving to carry thread back and forth.

gods, how they had deceived fair maidens, resorted to trickery, and appeared on earth from time to time in the form of poor and humble people. When the goddess saw this insult glowing in bright colors on Arachne's loom, she did not wait while the cloth was judged, but stepped forward, her gray eyes blazing with anger, and tore Arachne's work across. Then she struck Arachne across the face. Arachne stood there a moment, struggling with anger, fear, and pride. "I will not live under this insult," she cried, and seizing a rope from the wall, she made a noose and would have hanged herself.

The goddess touched the rope and touched the maiden. "Live on, wicked girl," she said. "Live on and spin, both you and your descendants. When men look at you they may remember that it is not wise to strive with Athene." At that the body of Arachne shriveled up, and her legs grew tiny, spindly, and distorted. There before the eyes of the spectators hung a little dusty brown spider on a slender thread.

All spiders descend from Arachne, and as the Greeks watched them spinning their thread wonderfully fine, they remembered the contest with Athene and thought that it was not right for even the best of men to claim equality with the gods.

TAKE NOTES

TAKE NOTES

Prologue from The Whale Rider

by Witi Ihimaera

In the old days, in the years that have gone before us, the land and sea felt a great emptiness, a yearning. The mountains were like a stairway to heaven, and the lush green rainforest was a rippling cloak of many colors. The sky was iridescent, swirling with the patterns of wind and clouds; sometimes it reflected the prisms of rainbow or southern aurora.[1] The sea was ever-changing, shimmering and seamless to the sky. This was the well at the bottom of the world, and when you looked into it you felt you could see to the end of forever.

This is not to say that the land and sea were without life, without vivacity. The tuatara, the ancient lizard with its third eye, was sentinel here, unblinking in the hot sun, watching and waiting to the east. The moa browsed in giant wingless herds across the southern island. Within the warm stomach of the rainforests, kiwi,[2] weka,[3] and the other birds foraged for *huhu* and similar succulent insects. The forests were loud with the clatter of tree bark, chatter of cicada, and murmur of fish-laden streams. Sometimes the forest grew suddenly quiet, and in wet bush could be heard the filigree of fairy laughter like a sparkling glissando.[4]

The sea, too, teemed with fish, but they also seemed to be waiting. They swam in brilliant shoals, like rains of glittering dust, throughout the greenstone depths—*hapuku, manga, kahawai, tamure, moki,* and *warehou*—herded by shark or *mango ururoa.* Sometimes from far off a white shape would be seen flying through the sea, but it would only be the serene

1. **southern aurora** (ô rôr′ ə) *n.* streamers or arches of light appearing above Earth in the Southern Hemisphere.
2. **kiwi** (kē′ wē) *n.* small, flightless New Zealand bird.
3. **weka** (wā′ kä) *n.* flightless New Zealand wading bird.
4. **glissando** (gli sän′ dō) *n.* quick sliding up or down the musical scale.

flight of the *tarawhai*, the stingray with the spike on its tail.

Waiting. Waiting for the seeding. Waiting for the gifting. Waiting for the blessing to come.

Suddenly, looking up at the surface, the fish began to see the dark bellies of the canoes from the east. The first of the Ancients were coming, journeying from their island kingdom beyond the horizon. Then, after a period, canoes were seen to be returning to the east, making long cracks on the surface sheen. The land and the sea sighed with gladness:

We have been found.

The news is being taken back to the place of the Ancients.

Our blessing will come soon.

In that waiting time, earth and sea began to feel the sharp pangs of need, for an end to the yearning. The forests sent sweet perfumes upon the eastern winds and garlands of *pohutukawa* upon the eastern tides.

The sea flashed continuously with flying fish, leaping high to look beyond the horizon and to be the first to announce the coming; in the shallows, the chameleon sea horses pranced at attention. The only reluctant ones were the fairy people, who retreated with their silver laughter to caves in glistening waterfalls.

The sun rose and set, rose and set. Then one day, at its noon apex, the first sighting was made. A spume on the horizon. A dark shape rising from the greenstone depths of the ocean, awesome, leviathan, breaching through the surface and hurling itself skyward before falling seaward again. Underwater the muted thunder boomed like a great door opening far away, and both sea and land trembled from the impact of that downward plunging.

Suddenly the sea was filled with awesome singing, a song with eternity in it, a song to the land:

You have called and I have come,
bearing the gift of the Gods.

The dark shape rising, rising again. A whale, gigantic. A sea monster. Just as it burst through the sea, a flying fish leaping high in its ecstasy saw water and air streaming like thunderous foam from that noble beast and knew, ah yes, that the time had come. For

TAKE NOTES

TAKE NOTES

the sacred sign was on the monster, a swirling tattoo imprinted on the forehead.

Then the flying fish saw that astride the head, as it broke skyward, was a man. He was wondrous to look upon, the whale rider. The water streamed away from him and he opened his mouth to gasp in the cold air. His eyes were shining with splendor. His body dazzled with diamond spray. Upon that beast he looked like a small tattooed figurine, dark brown, glistening, and erect. He seemed, with all his strength, to be pulling the whale into the sky.

Rising, rising. And the man felt the power of the whale as it propelled itself from the sea. He saw far off the land long sought and now found, and he began to fling small spears seaward and landward on his magnificent journey toward the land.

Some of the spears in midflight turned into pigeons, which flew into the forests. Others, on landing in the sea, changed into eels. And the song in the sea drenched the air with ageless music, and land and sea opened themselves to him, the gift long waited for: *tangata*, man. With great gladness and thanksgiving, the man cried out to the land,

Karanga mai, karanga mai, karanga mai.

Call me. But there was one spear, so it is told, the last, that, when the whale rider tried to throw it, refused to leave his hand. Try as he might, the spear would not fly.

So the whale rider uttered a prayer over the wooden spear, saying, "Let this spear be planted in the years to come, for there are sufficient spear already implanted. Let this be the one to flower when the people are troubled and it is most needed."

And the spear then leaped from his hands with gladness and soared through the sky. It flew across a thousand years. When it hit the earth, it did not change but waited for another hundred and fifty years to pass until it was needed.

The flukes of the whale stroked majestically at the sky.

Hui e, haumi e, taiki e.

Let it be done.

Grateful acknowledgment is made to the following for copyrighted material:

Atheneum Books for Young Readers, an imprint of Simon & Schuster "Stray" by Cynthia Rylant from *Every Living Thing.* Copyright © 1985 by Cynthia Rylant. Used by permission of Atheneum Books for Young Readers, an imprint of Simon & Schuster Children's Publishing Division.

Susan Bergholz Literary Services "Abuelito Who" by Sandra Cisneros from *My Wicked Wicked Ways.* Copyright © 1987 by Sandra Cisneros. Published by Third Woman Press and in hardcover by Alfred A. Knopf. Used by permission of Third Woman Press and Susan Bergholz Literary Services, New York.

John Brewton, George M. Blackburn & Lorraine A. Blackburn "Limerick (Accidents--More or Less Fatal)" from *Laughable Limericks.* Copyright © 1965 by Sara and John E. Brewton. Used by permission of Brewton, Blackburn and Blackburn.

Brooks Permissions "Cynthia In the Snow" from *Bronzeville Boys and Girls* by Gwendolyn Brooks. Copyright © 1956 by Gwendolyn Brooks. Used by consent of Brooks Permissions.

Curtis Brown Ltd. "Adventures of Isabel" by Ogden Nash from *Parents Keep Out.* Originally published by *Nash's Pall Mall Magazine.* Copyright © 1936 by Ogden Nash. All rights reserved.

Chronicle Books "Oranges" from *New and Selected Poems* by Gary Soto. Copyright © 1995 by Gary Soto. Visit www.chroniclebooks.com. Used with permission of Chronicle Books LLC, San Francisco.

Dell Publishing, a division of Random House, Inc. "The Tail" Copyright © 1992 by Joyce Hansen from *Funny You Should Ask* by David Gale, Editor. Used by permission of Dell Publishing, a division of Random House, Inc.

Dial Books for Young Readers, a division of Penguin Young Readers Group *Black Cowboy, Wild Horses* written by Julius Lester and illustrated by Jerry Pinkney. Text copyright © 1998 by Julius Lester. Illustrations copyright © 1998 by Jerry Pinkney. "Gluskabe and Old Man Winter: Abenaki" by Joseph Bruchac from *Pushing Up the Sky.* Copyright © 2000 by Joseph Bruchac, text. Used by permission of Dial Books for Young Readers, A Division of Penguin Young Readers Group, A Member of Penguin Group (USA).

Jean Grasso Fitzpatrick "The Ant and the Dove" by Leo Tolstoy from *Fables and Folktales Adapted from Tolstoy.* Translated by Jean Grasso Fitzpatrick. Used with permission.

Samuel French, Inc. "The Phantom Tollbooth" from *The Phantom Tollbooth: A Children's Play in Two Acts* by Susan Nanus and Norton Juster. Copyright © 1977 by Susan Nanus and Norton Juster. Used by permission of Samuel French, Inc. All rights reserved. CAUTION: Professionals and amateurs are hereby warned that "The Phantom Tollbooth," being fully protected under the copyright laws of the United States of America, the British Commonwealth countries, including Canada, and the other countries of the Copyright Union, is subject to royalty. All rights, including professional, amateur, motion picture, recitation, lecturing, public reading, radio, television and cable broadcasting, and the rights of translation into foreign languages, are strictly reserved. Any inquiry regarding the availability of performance rights, or the purchase of individual copies of the authorized acting edition, must be directed to Samuel French, Inc., 45 West 25th Street, NY, NY 10010 with other locations in Hollywood and Toronto, Canada.

Harcourt, Inc. "Ode to Family Photographs" from *Neighborhood Odes,* copyright © 1992 by Gary Soto. Used by permission of Harcourt, Inc.

HarperCollins Publishers, Inc. From *The Wounded Wolf* by Jean Craighead George. Text copyright © 1978 by Jean Craighead George. Used by permission of HarperCollins Publishers. "Langston Terrace" by Eloise Greenfield, from *Childtimes: A Three-Generation Memoir,* copyright © 1979 by Eloise Greenfield and Lessie Jones Little.

Harvard University Press "Fame Is a Bee" (#1763) by Emily Dickinson is used by permission of the publishers and the Trustees of Amherst College from *The Poems of Emily Dickinson,* Thomas H. Johnson, editor, Cambridge, Mass.: The Belknap Press of Harvard University Press, Copyright © 1951, 1955, 1979, 1983 by the President and Fellows of Harvard College.

The Barbara Hogenson Agency, Inc. "The Tiger Who Would Be King" by James Thurber, from *Further Fables for Our Time.* Copyright © 1956 James Thurber. Copyright © renewed 1984 by Rosemary A. Thurber. Used by arrangement with Rosemary A. Thurber and The Barbara Hogenson Agency, Inc.

Houghton Mifflin Company, Inc. "Arachne" from *Greek Myths.* Copyright © 1949 by Olivia E. Coolidge; copyright © renewed 1977 by Olivia E. Coolidge. Used by permission of Houghton Mifflin Company. All rights reserved.

Alfred A. Knopf Children's Books "Jackie Robinson: Justice at Last" from *25 Great Moments* by Geoffrey C. Ward and Ken Burns with S.A. Kramer, copyright © 1994 by Baseball Licensing International, Inc., "April Rain Song" from *The Collected Poems of Langston Hughes* by Langston Hughes, edited by Arnold Rampersad with David Roessel, Associate Editor, copyright © 1994 by The Estate of Langston Hughes.

Eve Merriam c/o Marian Reiner "Simile: Willow and Ginkgo" by Eve Merriam from *A Sky Full of Poems.* Copyright © 1964, 1970, 1973, 1986 by Eve Merriam. All rights reserved. Used by permission of Marian Reiner, Literary Agent, for the author.

Lillian Morrison c/o Marian Reiner "The Sidewalk Racer or On the Skateboard" by Lillian Morrison from *The Sidewalk Racer and Other Poems of Sports and Motion.* Copyright © 1965, 1967, 1968, 1977 by Lillian Morrison. Used by permission of Marian Reiner, for the author.

William Morrow & Company, Inc., a division of HarperCollins "The World is Not a Pleasant Place To Be" from *My House* by Nikki Giovanni. Copyright © 1972 by Nikki Giovanni. Used by permission of William Morrow & Company, Inc., a division of HarperCollins Publishers, Inc.

New Directions Publishing Corporation "Wind and Water and Stone" by Octavio Paz, translated by Eliot Weinberger, from *Collected Poems 1957–1987.* Copyright © 1984 by Octavio Paz and Eliot Weinberger. Used by permission of New Directions Publishing Corp.

Pearson Education *The Prince and the Pauper* Adapted from a book by Mark Twain, in Short Dramas and Teleplays. Copyright © 2000. Pearson Education, Inc., or its affiliates. Used by permission. All rights reserved.

Random House, Inc. "Life Doesn't Frighten Me" copyright © 1978 by Maya Angelou, from *And Still I Rise* by Maya Angelou. Used by permission of Random House, Inc.

Reed Publishing (NZ) Ltd. "Prologue from The Whale Rider" by Witi Ihimaera from *The Whale Rider.* Copyright © 1987 Witi Ihimaera. All rights reserved. Used by permission of Reed Publishing (NZ) Ltd.

Marian Reiner, Literary Agent "Haiku ("An old silent pond...")" by Matsuo Basho translated by Harry Behn from *Cricket Songs: Japanese Haiku.* Copyright © 1964 by Harry Behn.

University Press of New England "The Drive-In Movies" from *A Summer Life* copyright © 1990 by University Press of New England, Hanover, NH. Used by permission.

Viking Penguin, Inc. From *Zlata's Diary* by Zlata Filipovic from *Zlata's Life: A Child's Life in Sarajevo.* Translated by Christina Pribichevich-zoric. Copyright © 1994 Editions Robert Laffont/Fixot. Used by permission of Viking Penguin, a division of Penguin Group (USA) Inc.